FINDING GOD'S

THE MISSING PIECE

LEE EZELL

---

100 HUNTLEY STREET

SPECIAL EDITION

A ministry of
Crossroads Christian Communications Inc.

In Canada:

Crossroads Christian
Communications Inc.
100 Huntley Street
Toronto, Ontario
M4Y 2L1

Bus: (416) 961-8001

In the USA:

Crossroads Christian
Communications Inc.
Box 486
Niagara Falls, NY
14302

Prayer: (416) 961-1500

FINDING GOD'S PEACE FOR YOUR PAST

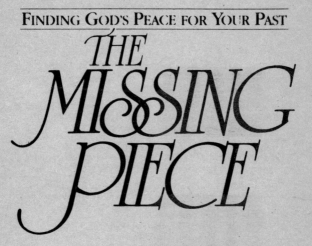

THE MISSING PIECE

LEE EZELL

BANTAM BOOKS

NEW YORK · TORONTO · LONDON · SYDNEY · AUCKLAND

THE MISSING PIECE

A Bantam Book / published by arrangement with the author

PRINTING HISTORY

Harvest House edition published 1986
Bantam edition / September 1988

Bantam Books are published by Bantam Books, a division of Bantam Doubleday Dell Publishing Group, Inc. Its trademark, consisting of the words "Bantam Books" and the portrayal of a rooster, is Registered in U.S. Patent and Trademark Office and in other countries. Marca Registrada, Bantam Books, 666 Fifth Avenue, New York, New York 10103

With Love
to my three daughters.
To Julie
whose birth awakened
my spiritual life
and to Pam and Sandi
who helped me live it out

Many thanks to Al Janssen
and Kin Millen
who helped piece together
the puzzle of this story.

This is a true story.
I have written it to offer hope
and stir the faith of those who need
to discover the Peace of God
for their missing pieces.

—LEE EZELL

Contents

THE MISSING PIECE

The Search

The blizzard grew worse as the afternoon wore on, delaying the arrival of the postman. The perpetual winter's ice on the country roads of Northern Michigan were covered by axle-deep snow. For several days a young mother, only two years out of high school, had restlessly awaited an envelope that would help her complete her search.

It really was a search; it couldn't be called an investigation—that was too official-sounding. She intended it to be systematic, persistent, and thoughtful. If it posed a threat to anyone, she would call it off.

While holding her daughter in one arm as she warmed a baby bottle on the stove with the other, Julie caught sight of the mailman as he stopped at the neighbor's mailbox up the road. Her pulse quickened. "Will it stop here?" she wondered. "Please, God, let this be the day. Sixty more seconds and I'll know."

The mailtruck plowed through the snow, throwing out a white wake until it stopped at the mailbox overhanging the side of the road. With boots, parka, and baby, Julie trudged through the snow out to the road, knowing that just because it stopped today didn't mean that ALMA was replying.

After pulling a fistful of mail out of the box, she stood and sorted it while the powder snow softly covered her and the baby. "There it is—Adoptees' Liberty Movement Association! Thank You, God."

Once again inside and sitting at the kitchen table,

she slit open the envelope, pulled out the four pages, and began reading: "WELCOME—we're pleased to hear from you! Our staff is made up of dedicated volunteers who have already completed their own searches. We are all aware of the enormous step you are about to take in beginning your search. We understand your feelings and your desire to know the truth of your origins."

As she began reading, her attention was interrupted by thoughts of her family who raised her and thoughts of her birthparents and what experiences this search could bring. She remembered back to when she was seven years old and learned she was "different"—a playmate had told her she was adopted. Just by the way it was tauntingly said, she sensed that "adopted" was not a warm term.

Throughout childhood her parents, during affectionate moments, would tell Julie she was special. She was the desire of their hearts, for she was chosen, but at the same time they never showed favoritism toward her or their other children. Did adoption really mean she was different? If so, how?

The mental image of her crying, running into the house to her mother, and asking what adoption meant played across her mind as if it were yesterday. Her mother had taken her on her lap and lovingly told her that adoption meant she was a special girl, a chosen daughter— certainly nothing to be ashamed of. Then she had asked her mother why her other mother gave her away. "Because you were loved," her mother had said. But at that age it was hard to understand.

And she *was* loved. No biological parents could have loved her more than her adoptive parents. Growing up in a home like this one—full of love, good family times, and mutual respect—was the perfect upbringing for any child. There were the childhood memories of a loving mom and dad, two protective older brothers who still teased her, many camping trips together, and church activities. Added to that, her parents indulged her by giving her many of her heart's desires—even her own horse. There was no doubt in Julie's mind that this was her family, the right family for her.

On this wintery afternoon Julie's excitement threatened to short-circuit her concentration. But she must not let it. She didn't want to hurt the important people in her life—her parents, her two brothers, her relatives, and her friends. She must think things through. What effect would this search have on them? Would they recognize her growing desire to know about her biological heritage? Could her family understand how important this was to her? Or would her actions make them feel rejected?

But Julie's natural curiosity about her biological tree could not be suppressed; it would only surface again. She wondered which of her personal characteristics were from nature and which from nurture. Questions about her birthmother would come to mind: "Is she alive? Could I ever have seen her? If so, it probably would have been in California before I moved. Do I look like her? Is she musical like me?

"Why was I given up? Were my parents married? Was my birthmother in school, and did she want to finish? Was she unable to make a home for me? Does she ever think of me on my birthday? Do I have any brothers or sisters? How much of me is inherited? No one can answer these questions but my birthmother." Although Julie lived with these uncertainties about her past and her identity, she never felt like a secondhand child. Yet this did not shut out the feeling that she had one hand covering one eye as she looked at her past.

Answers to these personal questions were not the only reason for Julie's quest. "There are things I want to say to my birthmother—Mom, I'm doing just fine. It's okay. I know it took courage for you to give me up. And it was the right decision. You gave me great parents."

After Julie married, her desire to know more about her biological background was heightened. She didn't want her children's history to be incomplete. And the birth of a daughter with red hair prompted new questions. Where did the red hair come from—her birthmother? Would she know some medical facts that could one day save herself or her daughter's life?

Julie was still concerned about the reaction of her adoptive family who had given her so much. In their quiet, unassuming way they had demonstrated Christian values, given her unconditional love, and provided a home life that prepared her to face adulthood. These thoughts caused Julie to smile. In some areas of her life she patterned herself after Mom—she even taught the primary girls' Sunday school class like Mom did when Julie was young.

Sounds of the baby awakening made Julie put aside her search packet. The rest of the afternoon was filled with the usual household tasks—attending to the baby and preparing the house for her husband to return from work.

When she saw the lights of his car reflecting off the white, snow-covered lane, Julie wanted to run out and share her news about the packet. But she knew that Bob was tired and wouldn't want to be bombarded with this news after work, so she stayed in the kitchen preparing the evening meal. After Bob had taken the baby out of the playpen, he came into the kitchen and greeted his wife with a kiss. Julie put her spoon down, grabbed him around the waist, nuzzled their baby, and told him the news.

"Bob, I got the search packet I ordered from ALMA. Do you want to see what's in it?"

"I had forgotten about it."

"Forgotten about it!"

"I married you for everything you are, not your ancestors. Of course I remember you writing the letter for it."

Julie walked over to the kitchen counter, where she had put the mail, and adding it to the folder containing her adoption papers she handed it to Bob, who sat at the kitchen table, playing with their baby. Julie spread out the papers on the table and explained them to Bob while the baby played at their feet.

"This should get us off to a good start," Bob said. He noticed something jotted with a pencil diagonally in the margin, clearly not part of the typed, official record. "Maybe these letters are a prefix of an old telephone number. It looks like they used to be written—with two letters and five digits."

Julie felt it was significant. "Bob, I'm not sure I want to start the search. What if I find out stuff I really don't want to know? What if my contact with my birthmother brings back sad memories and guilt to her? I don't want to ruin her life or disturb her family. On the other hand, what if I don't fit my mother's standards? What if she doesn't want to meet me and rejects me?"

"That's the chance you'll have to take," replied Bob. "But you don't have to meet her. You can stop anywhere along the way without upsetting her life. A name and medical history from the adoption agency could be enough. Who knows—maybe she's not even alive."

"This is something we'll have to think about," mused Julie out loud. With that she put the papers in a kitchen drawer and went back to preparing supper.

Winter days blurred together as Julie would occasionally run across a magazine article, book, or a television interview showing how other adoptees went about their searches. During the following months she and her husband prayed for guidance, and gradually the doubts and negative feelings about the risks they faced were replaced with confidence and the courage to act. She made phone calls, wrote letters, and gathered information on her own from lawyers and from the hospital where she was born.

Now that she was more at ease with her decision, new thoughts began to creep into Julie's mind. She sensed a deep urge to tell her birthmother about the driving force in her life. Julie wondered how she would express

5

this to a person whom she had never met, yet cared for. If she found her natural mother, she didn't want her words or actions to turn her away.

Julie's spirit wrestled with the risk. She didn't want to lose her adoptive mother, but whenever she had doubts, another thought would come to the fore: "True love is willing to risk loss and rejection." That rededication rekindled the resolve to continue the search.

In December of 1984, nearly a year after she received the packet from ALMA, Julie once more leafed through all the records. The old telephone number caught her attention: The moment had arrived. With renewed confidence, yet still nervous, Julie picked up the phone and dialed the 20-year-old number.

1

The Great Escape

An ordinary Greyhound bus was supposed to be my magic carpet to a new life. I let the wind blow on my face through a small opening in the window as I watched fields green with crops of corn and wheat pass by. Next to me, my mother leaned her seat back and tried to catch some sleep while across the aisle my two younger sisters, Kay and Sue, giggled as they played with a cheap plastic game they had bought at the last stop.

I felt like a prisoner breaking the chains of confinement and experiencing her first moments of freedom. For 17 years I had endured the tyranny of my father, but now, in June of 1962, I could finally take charge of my own life. Though we had been on the road for only 30 hours, the Philadelphia we had left seemed like another world.

I thought of the dreary rain that had fallen as we headed for the bus station carrying all our possessions in just a few bags. It reflected our lives in a bleak inner-city section of Philadelphia—"the City of Brotherly Shove," we called it. We had lived in a tiny rowhouse that my mother's parents owned, where she had been born and raised. Our neighborhood was a colorful mixture of second-generation immigrants—Italian, Irish, German, and Polish—each seemingly trying to outshout the other as we all struggled to survive.

My father had once told me that his greatest wish in life was to have a son. After five swings and misses, he admitted striking out and gave up. Each of the five Kinney daughters received one simple three-letter name—Zoe, Ann, Lee, Kay, and Sue. In our home, each family member was on her own to do or die, sink or swim. If we could succeed on our own, fine. But we were not to expect help from our parents or anyone else.

At 14 I had started working at after-school jobs to help with expenses at home. My first job was at the neighborhood variety store, cutting oilcloth that hung from rolls on the wall. For this I was paid a cherished 25 cents an hour. My escape from the pressures of home came through music and drama. I had played the violin in school orchestras and a string quartet, sung in numerous choral groups, and acted the lead role in several musical comedies. I frequented Dick Clark's American Bandstand, where I could dance away my misery with other Bandstand "regulars."

I would have to do much more than that now that I had graduated from high school. My two older sisters, Zoe and Ann, had managed to find their men and escape to San Francisco and Cincinnati. Now the rest of us were moving west to join Zoe in California. Once again doubts flooded my mind. Were we doing the right thing? Should we have left my father the way we did? Would I now become responsible for the welfare of the family? How would my Eastern-born-and-reared mother adjust to life in California? There was no turning back now, yet I couldn't help but wonder if I would have any regrets.

No! Nothing could be worse than what we had left behind. If my father's rampage six weeks earlier had been a single incident, perhaps I could have forgiven him. By day my father was a housepainter; by night he was a recluse in a basement papered with pornographic pictures. There in the confinement of that dim cellar he would try to drink his way into oblivion. After hours of drinking, with inhibitions lowered and tongue loosened, he would emerge from the cellar with a demonized look on his face. It was as though he was a wild man leaping off the screen of a horror movie as he began to beat any family member near him. Then he would turn on anyone who tried to break it up, and would finish the tantrum by turning on my mother, who always endured the worst beatings.

My father's alcoholic explosions caused all of us to develop disappearing acts. My secret hiding places were under my bed and behind the clothes that hung in the dining room closet. But none of us could escape every time. One evening my father emerged from the basement with a cat-o'-nine-tails he had fashioned out of a broom handle and leather straps sliced from his old belts. That produced the worst beatings, and as I entered high school it was not unusual for me and my sisters to attend school with concealed bruises from the rampage of the night before.

On three occasions the violence was so bad that I had called the police. Unfortunately, they didn't like the domestic violence that was so common in our neighborhood any more than I did, and they only answered one of my three calls. It was on the final unanswered call, just six weeks before my high school graduation, that I determined I had had enough. As Dad retreated from his latest round of fury, I had yelled to Mom, "I'm getting out of here!"

A couple days later I had told Mom that I was serious. "As soon as I graduate, I'm leaving."

"And where do you think you'll go?" she had snapped.

"Maybe I'll go live with Zoe in California. I wish you and Kay and Sue would come with me. Why should they continue to suffer? They don't deserve it, and neither do you."

"I can't leave. What would your father do without me? Besides, I've lived here all my life."

"Mom, we've *got* to leave. Someday he's going to kill you." She had just turned away, unable to face the awful truth. So I had called my sister and made the arrangements for us to go. Zoe had said she would help us find an apartment and jobs. An auctioneer came through the house and bought all of our old, broken-down furniture. Mom must have told my father the news, and somehow she managed to vacate the only home she had ever known.

"Lee, look! The Mississippi River!" Kay's enthusiastic squeal interrupted my thoughts. For Kay and Sue this was an adventure. They were too young to feel the responsibility of having to provide for the family. If this plan failed, I was to blame, for I was the one who had pushed us to move. They were free to enjoy the scenery that brought their grade-school geography lessons to life. Already we had passed through Harrisburg, Cleveland, Toledo, and Chicago. Shortly we would be crossing the Great Plains on our way to the Rockies.

A few minutes later we were pulling into another town. My mother stirred as the driver downshifted. As she saw the blue neon sign proclaiming "Bus Depot" glide past my window, she wordlessly grabbed for her purse and rose to stretch her legs. She gave me and each of my sisters a quarter as we entered the waiting room. There had to be a hundred and one things to do with a quarter—get your picture taken, eat at the vending machine, use the phone. The girls hurried off to spend their fortune on some candy bars while Mom and I wandered aimlessly.

Several of the benches were occupied by sleeping drifters, with remains of their bottles of cheap wine strewn on the floor. It looked as though they had never recovered from the Great Depression. An old man in a tattered trench coat spotted us and said, "Excushe me, ma'am. Could you shpare a dime for a cup of coffee?" Mom walked on, ignoring him, but I stopped, for in his unshaven face I was reminded of my father. Would my father wind up on the streets, a hopeless bum begging for some loose change? Quickly I reached into my pocket, pulled out my quarter, and dropped it into his hand. I would do without a candy bar this time.

A few moments later we reboarded our bus. "Mom, did you tell Dad where we were going?" I asked as we settled into our seats.

"Yes," she answered without looking at me.

"What's he going to do now?"

"I don't know," she said as she again reclined her seat and closed her eyes. I could tell from the way she tried to hide her tears that she couldn't talk about it. Though she knew this was the best for her and her daughters, she was ashamed to admit that her marriage was a failure. Hers was a cruel dilemma: She was emotionally dependent on her husband, yet unable to live with him. Her distress made me determined to never be so "weak."

My own bitterness was diminishing the further we got from Philadelphia. As the bus returned to the highway, I reflected on the hopelessness of that bum to whom I had given my quarter. He was just like my father . . . a victim. Like many other people in our neighborhood, my father resented his lot in life but had no release. What dreams he might have harbored had disappeared early in life. What few opportunities he had had were blown. His unresolved anger eventually changed his personality, and the effects of alcohol exaggerated that change. My understanding the situation didn't change the fact that I couldn't stand to live with him. But it did motivate me to pray.

I prayed a lot on that transcontinental trip, especially when I began to worry. It was the only way to cope with the uncertainty. The plan was to live with Zoe and her family until we could find an apartment. Both Mom and I would have to work. She was a legal secretary, and I had taken typing and shorthand courses in high school. "Lord, please help us find work," I prayed, and again I felt the reassurance that God heard me.

It hadn't always been that way. For years what little religious influence I had was received at an old Gothic-style church. During the liturgy, beams of sunlight would filter through the stained-glass windows and make me

11

feel holy. It gave me goose bumps. There seemed to be a mystery surrounding the ceremony. Only an occasional echo of a whisper or noise would break the silence in that dim nave. This was God's house, where I supposed He lived, in His invisible way, with His Son and the Holy Ghost—the One who gave you those goose bumps.

I had to chuckle now as I thought of those primitive concepts of God that I had accepted without question. My idea of God was built around my own notions and what a few other people had said. I thought that if I could tilt the scales by doing a little more good than bad, I could go straight to heaven, avoiding hell and skipping purgatory. But I had no way of knowing what my score was. Even though I was making up the rules as I went along, there was a gap between my beliefs and my practice. Apart from the weekly hour in "God's house," I had no relationship with God at all.

Though I didn't understand it at the time, God was working out His plan for my life. It was certainly evident that fateful night when two girlfriends and I could not find a fourth girl for pinochle. We decided to attend an evangelistic crusade at the convention center for entertainment, and maybe even a few laughs. The preacher was a man I had never heard of—Billy Graham.

I could still vividly recall that night. Billy Graham's message caught me off-guard—it was so simple. He explained that the Bible portrayed God not as a heavenly policeman or harsh judge, but as a loving Father who loved the world so much that He gave us His only Son. Whoever believed in the Son, Jesus Christ—who died for our sins and rose again from the dead—would have eternal life.

There was no way I could do enough good things to qualify for heaven. God had made it clear that those who received Christ qualified, and the rest were sinners, separated from God forever. It was a black-and-white situation. One thing was for certain—I wasn't "in" Christ. Therefore I was a sinner. I had always thought of sin as stealing or other bad things, but now I realized that sin was simply refusing to accept God's provision. The Bible said that everyone has sinned, but also that anyone who received Christ could be forgiven and accepted by God as righteous, no matter how badly they had sinned.

That night I surrendered my life to God. With hundreds of people I made my way to the front of the auditorium. A counselor encouraged me as I prayed and accepted Christ as my Savior. "Dear God, thank You for sending Your Son, Jesus Christ, to die on the cross and pay for my sins. I now believe in You and accept You as my Lord and Savior. In Jesus' name, Amen." It was so simple, yet so profound. Together we read some verses from the Bible, and she took my name and address so I could begin receiving a correspondence course.

I knew this was the beginning of a new life for me. As I rode the subway home I kept thinking of the verse the counselor had read that said I was a new person— that old things were passed away, that all things had become new. Somehow I envisioned that happening at home. Things were going to be different. Dad would change, and we would become a happy family. That fantasy lasted until I arrived home and tried to open the front door. My dad had passed out in front of it, and I had to push with all my strength to get past him. I could still remember my disappointment, thinking, "Wait a minute, God. This isn't what I signed up for. Nothing's new here."

But my *life* was new, for I was talking to God in a real way for the first time. I now had a relationship with God, not a religion. I no longer had to wait for church to pray. I could talk with Him on the subway, or in school, or while lying in my bed at night. God wasn't changing my external circumstances, but He was making some internal changes in me. I no longer felt alone.

I talked with God a lot on our four-day bus trip. As we left Sacramento and headed down the last stretch of road toward our new home, I admired the wide-open spaces and the warm sunshine that seemed to offer promise of a new life free from pain. "Lord, we're beginning over. I know You're going to take care of us and everything will be all right. Thank You for taking us out of Philadelphia."

The windows of the bus were wide open as we felt the heat of the Sacramento Valley. I looked over at Mom and grinned. "It's going to be great out here!" She didn't say anything, but wiped her face with a handkerchief. Then I noticed it wasn't just sweat. There were tears in her eyes. "Mom, why are you crying?"

She just shook her head. "I don't know why I let you talk me into moving. There's nothing here but palm trees and surfboards and a bunch of wild people with crazy ideas."

Ignoring her misconceptions of California, I reminded her, "But just think, no cold winters. No more leggins and boots and heavy sweaters. We won't have to shovel snow."

"Lee, you make it sound so good. You don't understand."

She was right—I didn't understand. And I felt if she didn't adjust, it was my fault. I tried to reassure her. "You'll be happy here. You'll be glad we moved."

We were quiet as we headed into San Francisco and caught our first glimpse of the Golden Gate Bridge. To me it symbolized that here was the land of opportunity. No one would beat us here. We would make some money and live a good life. I would find the man of my dreams here, and my miserable childhood in Philadelphia would fade into a distant memory.

As we pulled into the bus station, I could see Zoe waiting for us. She had made it here, and we would too. Mom seemed to perk up at the sight of her oldest daughter. In a moment we were embracing, and I couldn't help thinking, "Lee, this is it. Just think, in a few weeks you'll be 18 years old! What a great time for everything to come together! Sure, there will be a few adjustments, but nothing you can't handle."

2

The Doris Day Fantasy

"Five minutes to lunchtime!" Barb reminded us, motivating me to give one final burst of energy before our break. It had been several months since we had arrived in San Francisco. I had found my first "real" job as a secretary for a small sailboat manufacturer. Having a responsible job made me feel important and accepted as an adult.

Zoe had graciously put up with the four of us at her home for a few weeks until we got settled. After both Mom and I found work, we had moved to a small two-bedroom apartment a few blocks away from my sister and her family. However, I was distressed to find that while we had escaped from the wrath of our alcoholic father, my sisters and I did not enjoy total peace. There were frequent shouting matches with Mom, and I noticed with embarrassment that such arguments were not the norm in our new neighborhood. We had changed our environment, but the environment hadn't changed us.

Fortunately I had an escape from the cramped apartment. I had joined the USO and was active in helping to organize parties, shows, and dances for soldiers at military bases around the San Francisco Bay area. It gave me a chance to use some of my creative energy, especially my love for drama and music, and to meet a lot of

17

nice young men. I wasn't particularly eager to get serious with any one man, but the experience of meeting men from around the country had removed some of the cynicism of my past. I was determined to be a bright, outgoing, sanguine woman who enjoyed being the life of the party. I was willing to be carefree and trusting of the people who came into my life.

"Lunchtime!" said Barb. I quickly turned off my typewriter, grabbed my brown-bag lunch, and headed with Barb to the small conference room that also served as our coffee-break room and lunchroom. Barb was a divorcee in her midtwenties who had worked for the company nearly two years. The third secretary was Jean, an older married woman. She was on the phone and motioned that she would join us in a few minutes.

"What a busy morning!" said Barb as she poured herself a cup of coffee and sat down.

"I'll say. That's one large order we've got to process, and I still have to get the boss's letters typed."

Jean came in and announced as she sat down, "Bad news. We've got to work late tonight."

"Oh, no, not again," Barb groaned. Ours was a small, struggling company with only 20 employees. So we all had multiple responsibilities.

"It's that large order you're working on," Jean explained. "They're shipping the boats out tonight and we've got to finish the paperwork."

"Oh, well, at least it's not Friday," I laughed.

"And what's happening Friday?" asked Barb. "Got a big date?"

"I'm helping put on a USO dance over in Oakland."

"Great! Why don't you line me up with someone?"

"What do you have in mind?" I asked, realizing that we were playing another of our lunch-hour dating games.

Jean ate quietly while Barb dreamily recited, "Oh, make him about six-foot-three. Strong. Tanned. It's okay if he looks like Burt Lancaster."

"I'll see what I can do," I said with a laugh.

Jean mentioned that she thought it was great that I

would take the time to volunteer for the USO. "There are a lot of other things you could do with your time."

"I enjoy it," I said. "I really appreciate these men who are preparing to fight for our country. Many of them are homesick. Some of them wish they had never signed up. Others miss their girlfriends at home. They need someone just to listen and show them a good time."

"Do you use your accents?"

"Si, last week I geeve them my Spanish accent." Then in a deeper voice I continued, "Dis veek, ve could be a 'sexy' Sveed, ya? But too bad I don't have the voluptuous body to go with that accent."

Barb laughed at my quick transition from a Spanish accent to a thick Swedish accent. Studying language and ethnic accents had always been my hobby. Then Barb asked, "Do you have a favorite guy?"

"No, I try to remain neutral and dance with all of them."

"Have you gone out with any of the guys—you know, behind the annex and . . ." she raised her eyebrows a couple of times. I knew what she meant.

"Barb, I'm not that kind of girl. I'm saving myself for marriage."

"You lose," said Barb, shaking her head. "I gave up on that idea years ago."

"Well, I haven't. I'm still a virgin and I'm going to stay that way until I get married."

"Good for you," said Jean. "I wish I'd had your determination when I was your age. Unfortunately, most men have only one thing on their minds."

I knew what she meant, thinking again of the magazine pictures that had lined my father's basement. From those graphic pictures and the coarse jokes he told around his friends, I had learned at an innocent age that many men considered a woman as little more than a sexual object. Still, I held out hope that some man might see me as someone who was witty and intelligent . . . *and* good-looking.

I told the two women about the time I had said to

my mother, "I can't decide if it's better to have beauty or brains." Mom had had a snappy comeback: "Never forget, Honey, it's better to have beauty because men can *see* clearer than they can *think*."

Jean and Barb laughed with me, partly because of the silly way I imitated my mother's thick Philadelphia accent. "Well, your mother's partly right," Jean said. "But there are some good men out there. You stick to your principles and wait. The right man will come along soon enough."

"I know. Someday my Prince Charming is going to come riding by. I just hope I don't have to clean up after his horse!" And with that joke we all laughed and headed back to work. I didn't tell them my full dream—that I was going to be like Doris Day. She was always so cute and friendly in the movies, and nothing naughty ever happened to her. If Hollywood could portray such a "live-happily-ever-after" message, then certainly I could experience it, especially if I really believed it with all my heart.

Late that afternoon, in the yard where the sailboats were stored adjacent to the office, two men began loading boats on a truck. The older of the two was Jack, one of our traveling salesmen who appeared in our office only occasionally. He had stopped in briefly to review the paperwork before beginning the loading process. He was a rather unrefined, even crude man. His face was conspicuous by his greasy forehead framed by an untrimmed beard. Plus he was overweight by at least 100 pounds.

It was nearly seven when the last of the boats was loaded on the truck. Jean, Barb, and I were finishing the invoices and other papers as the two men came into the office. Without looking up I commented, "I'm sure glad we're almost done. In half an hour there's an old Cary Grant movie on TV. I love those old movies."

"That sounds like a great way to relax," said Jack. "Why don't you all pick up a pizza and come over to my house and we'll watch the movie together."

I shrugged my shoulders and said, "Sure, why not?" Watching a movie with friends sounded better than going home to my crowded, tension-filled apartment.

Motioning to Barb and Jean, he said, "You two girls know the way, so why don't you pick up the pizza? Lee, you can follow me in your car."

A few minutes later I was slowly following Jack through an area of old industrial buildings. We turned left and right several times and I began to feel that we were wandering aimlessly. Then we crossed a four-lane thoroughfare into a neighborhood characterized by old, deteriorating homes that surrounded a trailer park that time had seemed to forget.

Jack pulled into a driveway of an ancient-looking aluminum house trailer and parked under a flat roof that sagged so that it nearly scraped the top of his car. "That's what he probably calls his carport," I thought sarcastically. "This does look like the house that Jack would build." It was a grimy-looking trailer with paint curling upward like flower petals from the aluminum siding. The front "lawn" was nothing more than hard-packed dirt. "That's all right," I muttered to myself as I parked behind Jack. "I'm no stranger to run-down places."

I got out and followed Jack up two wooden steps and through the front door. Once inside, Jack fought the warped door until it closed. Then he switched on the television set as he asked me what channel the movie was on.

Exhausted and ready to relax, I slumped into a beat-up chair that (like all the other furniture) was threadbare and had stuffing showing in the most worn spots. Jack fiddled with the rabbit ears until the snow was gone from the black-and-white picture. Then he turned and, fixing his eyes on me, began to cross the room. "I'm glad my friends will be here in a few minutes," I thought.

Jack stopped in front of me, then bent over, yanked me from my chair, and kissed me on my neck. It was so sudden and unexpected that it took a moment to realize his intentions. "No!" I yelled as I fought to push him away. "No! No! No!" I yelled repeatedly.

Although familiar with abuse, I had never been sexually assaulted. I was so naive to the ways of the world that even while I fought, part of my mind questioned why this unkempt, unattractive middle-aged man was doing this. What had I done to encourage him? And where were the other gals? Shouldn't they be here by now?

"Stop doing this to me!" I yelled as Jack wrestled me onto the couch. His attack resurrected the awful memories from deep within, the trapped feelings from the times when my father in an alcoholic stupor would beat me without reason. Once again I felt that sense of no control. My screams turned into cries of helplessness as Jack ripped off my undergarments. While crying out from fear and pain, I heard Jack mutter in disgust, "Oh, no, a virgin." In my tormented mind I wondered how he could continue the violation of my body and soul if he was dissatisfied.

It was over quickly. My rapist tumbled to the floor, satiated, seemingly no longer aware of me. Fear and rage caused my heart to pound. The fight, the adrenaline shooting through my body, and the emotional agony of it all left me drenched in perspiration. I struggled to my feet, pulled down my dress, grabbed my shoes and purse, and ran for the door. Fearing he might try to stop me, I felt a surge of strength as I yanked open the door and rushed across the hard dirt to my car. Without looking back, I started the car and hurried out of the trailer park.

I didn't slow down until I was within a few blocks of my home. Then the full impact of what had happened overwhelmed me. I pulled onto a side street, parked under a tree, and began sobbing hysterically. Guilt welled up within me as I told myself, "You're an idiot! Why did you go to his place alone? You were asking for trouble. You should have known better."

As I buried my face in my hands and sobbed into

the steering wheel, my mind was a jumble of thoughts. I was furious at having my innocent sexuality savagely ripped from me. During all these years of boyfriends and dating I had held out . . . for this? I had been robbed in body and soul.

I slid down in the driver's seat of my car, hoping the darkness would hide me from the view of families who sat laughing in front of their TV's. Fear blanketed me and I sat frozen in this position for at least an hour. What would I do when Jack came to the office again? How could I tell anyone? I was afraid this large, powerful man would take revenge.

But who could I tell, anyway? Who would believe me? People would think I had seduced him. Besides, it would be humiliating just to realize that others knew.

I could tell the police, but what would my mother think? She would never accept it. Besides, I had just turned 18, and somewhere I'd heard you couldn't prosecute for rape after a girl turned 18. So what good would it do to tell the police?

This can't be happening to me, I thought. This just can't be true. It's only a bad dream.

"Tough it out, Lee," my racing mind told me. "You've been through worse than this. You'll get over it. Just don't let anyone else know."

But I could tell someone. I could tell God. "Why?" I cried out in the solitude of my car. "Why me? Where were *You* when this happened? Why didn't You warn me? Haven't I suffered enough? Are You punishing me for something? Are You a sadist who enjoys zapping helpless little people like me? I really thought things would be different now that I had Jesus in my life."

My emotional outburst seemed to calm me down. I had to try to push those unanswerable questions back into my subconscious. "Get yourself together," I said to myself. "Go home. Go to bed. You'll forget this ever happened." I decided then that this attack would be a secret that would go with me to my grave.

With that I started my car and headed for home. But as I drove I realized that while I might succeed in hiding this secret from the world, a huge hole had been drilled in my life. My Doris Day fantasy was forever dashed. A piece of me had been rudely ripped out of my life, and nothing could ever fill it.

3

No Place to Hide

No one looked up as I opened the front door of the apartment. In the darkened living room, my mother and sisters were preoccupied with some television program. I quickly slipped down the hall to the bedroom I shared with my 13-year-old sister Kay, grabbed a nightgown, then entered the bathroom and locked the door. I now felt an intense need to rid my body of the guilt and the sense of feeling dirty. As I stripped off my soiled clothes, I wanted to throw them away, for they would always remind me of this awful night. But I knew I wouldn't be able to explain that.

My "recovery room" became the shower. I let the warm water pour over me and soothe my hurting body. However, the water could not wash away the emotions of a broken soul. Safe for a moment in the noise of the shower, I let the tears flow. With those tears, it was as if the youth of my life ran out of me.

I was lonely, guilty, dirty, full of fear. It had been a long time since I had known that helpless feeling of being controlled physically by a man. Resentment was beginning to seethe in me like a rumbling volcano. "Chastity should not be a luxury for a woman," I thought. How I longed for loving arms to surround me and allow me to cry my heart out! I needed someone to comfort me, a person who was sympathetic and understanding.

As I washed my defiled body, uncontrollable sobs escaped from my soul and became part of the cleansing water. When I finished washing, I stood under the warm water as long as possible. Finally, to avoid any questions from my mother and sisters, I forced myself to turn off the water. As I dried myself, the bath towel felt almost too heavy to lift and pull over my body. Each normally effortless task consumed all of my concentration and energy. When I finished drying, I slipped into my cool cotton nightgown, shuffled to my room, and fell into bed. The blankets formed a cocoon around me, isolating me from the world. But they couldn't protect me from my turbulent emotions.

I pretended to sleep when Kay finally came to bed, then tossed and turned most of the night, reliving the horror of the event. How desperately I had wanted to escape. But escape was impossible. "Why me, God?" I cried again and again, this time not so much in anger as in a desire to make sense of the emptiness in my life that seemed like a gaping hole.

How could I trust anyone again? Maybe I needed to learn my lesson and realize that I just couldn't trust people. I had relaxed too much. I felt ashamed. No, stupid. I should never have gone to Jack's trailer. I didn't even know him. It was shocking to realize that I had felt no apprehension. "You'd better stop being so naive," I told myself. "Watch where you go. Check people's motives. Don't think that everyone is your brother or sister."

That pep talk might help prevent another tragedy, but it couldn't repair the present damage. There was no place to turn except to God. There were no other options. Somehow He would have to give me answers. I didn't want to go through life always mistrusting people's motives, but neither could I bear the thought of suffering any more meaningless pain. On the desk by my bed was the latest study in my correspondence Bible course from Billy Graham. Every time I did the lesson and sent it in, I felt good. More than reading a pop psychology book, the Bible was offering me some solid practical principles I could lean on. I gained strength from its pages. The lessons covered basic principles that were easy to understand and apply to my life. When I completed a study, I would send it in so someone could correct it, and then get it back a few weeks later with some encouraging words and a new study. As I finally drifted into a light sleep, I determined that I would do the new lesson the next evening after work.

The next morning nothing seemed different around the apartment. As I drove to work, stopping on the way for a doughnut and cup of coffee, I wondered how people around me could be unaware of "the event" and my despairing feelings. But the world continued turning as if nothing had ever happened. At the office, neither Barb nor Jean acted as if they even remembered the conversation at the end of work the previous evening. I wondered if they could tell by looking at me . . . did I look raped? Did my face reveal the turbulence of the night before? Did they pick up signals that something had happened to me, that I was different?

By lunchtime I couldn't stand it any longer. Trying to sound nonchalant, I finally asked, "Hey, what happened to you guys last night? I thought you were picking up pizza and coming over to Jack's."

"It was too late," said Jean. "I had to get home. I thought *you* went, Barb."

"I didn't feel like going," said Barb. "I was too tired."

They didn't ask about what I'd done, and as Barb changed the subject I suddenly realized that they had never made any commitment to Jack. Maybe I had just assumed they would come, while they had thought it was something they could do if they felt like it, but it was no big deal. I couldn't talk about it any further without revealing my problem. I needed to bury this bizarre incident that never should have happened.

My one remaining concern was what to do when

Jack came back to the office. He had left early that morning with the load of boats and wasn't due back in the office for a couple of months. What would I say to him the next time I saw him? "I'll just ignore him," I decided. "If I don't pay any attention to him, it will be over." I had to force myself to go on with business as usual.

Somehow I survived that day at work, with my mind suspended between reality and a nightmare. My emotions were so on edge that I knew I could not face my mother and sisters. I had to gain some control over my life. Once during dinner Mom noticed that I was unusually quiet. "I'm not feeling well," I mumbled. "I think I'll go to bed early." Fortunately, my mother and sisters were wrapped up in their own worlds and didn't pay any further attention to me.

As soon as the table was cleared, I isolated myself in my room and opened the Bible study from the Billy Graham Evangelistic Association. Before my experience at the crusade, I had thought of the Bible only as a musty old book that graced the lectern in a Gothic church. But after doing these studies over the past months I had come to realize that the Bible was filled with truth against which I could measure my life and find direction. Now it was my only hope. The studies had always been such a help, so I plunged in eagerly.

The printed Scripture at the start of the lesson immediately caught my attention.

> Delight thyself also in the Lord, and he shall
> give thee the desires of thine heart. Commit
> thy way unto the Lord; trust also in him, and
> he shall bring it to pass.[1]

The word "commit" really stuck. I needed to turn this experience over to God. There had to be a moment in time when I definitely committed this assault to Him. I couldn't just treat it with a "Que sera sera—Whatever will be, will be" attitude. And I couldn't just feel sorry for myself and have a pity party. I needed to do something positive: Commit it to God's care. The verse promised that He would take care of it from there and make everything work out.

Most of the study's assigned Scripture readings were from the New Testament. I particularly enjoyed the stories of Jesus and His parables. The epistles were a little harder to understand. This evening two of the passages were from Paul's second letter to the Corinthians. The thoughts of "Why me, God?" were unrelenting until I read about some of the things that the apostle Paul endured. I started to cry as I read, and with the tears came God's comfort pouring into my heart. "Five times I received from the Jews thirty-nine lashes. Three times I was beaten with rods, once I was stoned, three times I was shipwrecked, a night and a day I have spent in the deep."[2] He went on to list many other dangers he encountered. It was obvious that Paul, for all his godliness, didn't escape problems.

The clear answer to my question "Why me, God?" was "Why *not* you, Lee? Why should *you* be exempt?" Why should anyone be exempt? Paul had all kinds of problems, but he was able to write, "We are afflicted in every way, but not crushed; perplexed, but not despairing; persecuted, but not forsaken; struck down, but not destroyed."[3]

As I continued to read, I realized that Paul went to jail and suffered all kinds of injustices and unfair treatment, and yet he survived. Who was I to think I deserved some special treatment? In my limited way I began to consider that God could give me the same spirit He had given to Paul. Possibly He could even begin to fill in the gaping void that caused my intense pain.

With that perspective I felt confident in committing my situation to God. In the following days I often recommitted it to Him as the awful memories would resurface. "Lord, help me endure this pain" was my simple prayer, and many times that was the only thing that helped maintain my sanity.

* * *

As the days passed and some of my pain and confusion subsided, I noticed that I had a growing suspicion and mistrust toward all men. Before, I was always somewhat hesitant to enter into any significant relationship; now I kept everyone even further away. I continued my USO activities, but stopped dating entirely. I enjoyed trying to bring some happiness to the guys who were serving their country; they were like the brothers I had never had. With so many unresolved questions and fears, I was determined to limit myself only to those brother-sister relationships. I knew that eventually I would begin dating again, but for now I put it out of my mind. It would take time to regain the trust I would need in order to be comfortable in a dating situation.

As the next few weeks passed, I began experiencing a sore throat and nausea, as if I were coming down with the flu. "The bug's going around," Barb said one day when I complained. I struggled at work for several days, never feeling sick enough to stay home. Then one morning I woke up feeling totally exhausted. Thinking that I needed some extra rest to shake the flu, I phoned in sick. But after two days in bed, I didn't feel any better.

Finally I decided to go to the doctor, hoping for an antibiotic that could get me back on the job. A nurse listened to my symptoms and took blood and urine samples. Then the doctor came in and gave me a routine physical exam.

"Have you had any congestion in your nose or ears?" he asked as he applied a stethoscope to my back.

"No, just a sore throat," I answered.

"How long have you felt nauseous?"

"A couple of weeks."

"Have you had any vomiting or diarrhea?"

"I've thrown up a couple of times in the morning. I don't feel like eating much of anything."

"When did you have your last period?"

I thought this was a strange question. What did this have to do with the flu? I had to think for a moment before I answered, "About two months."

"Have you had intercourse?"

I swallowed hard, then answered, "Uh, not really." The doctor gave me a strange look. "Well, I mean . . . once," I stammered.

"How long ago?"

"Six weeks." I was tempted to tell him that I was raped, but something stopped me. Maybe I thought he would call the police. There would be questions. What would my mother think? She would be so embarrassed. I had to handle it as best I could and move on.

"Well, you're probably not expecting this," the doctor said. "I don't know if it's good news or bad. But as far as I can tell, you're pregnant. I'm sure the blood test will confirm it when we get the results back in a couple of days."

"But that's not possible!" I protested. "No, it just can't be." I felt like I was entering the Twilight Zone. "A person can't get pregnant if she's a virgin. I mean, she can't get pregnant the first time. It's a medical impossibility. Right?"

The doctor, with a crude cordiality, explained, "On the contrary, it's quite possible. You were in the middle of your menstruation cycle. That's when a woman ovulates. If intercourse occurs during that time when a woman is fertile, she can become pregnant." That was news to me. Here I was a high school graduate, supposedly "educated." But my sex education had stopped at the kindergarten level of information. I knew there was a monthly menstruation cycle, but no one—not my mother, girlfriends, or teachers—had ever explained ovulation to me before.

"There are several options available to you," the doctor continued. "We can discuss them now or at your next appointment."

I just shook my head, trying to deny what I'd heard. The doctor closed his file and said, "Let's wait. You obviously need some time to think about it."

In shock, I managed to find my way back to the car. Once again I sought security within this old battered vehicle. I drove to a quiet tree-lined street where I could sob without anyone noticing me. My mind tried to deny what I had just heard, but feelings of utter despair surged up with the persistent thought, "This *can't* be happening. It's not possible! How can I, an unwanted child, be pregnant with an unwanted child?"

After half an hour the tears began to subside. I forced myself to review the facts. I had missed my period. I did have the symptoms of morning sickness. The rape had occurred in the middle of my cycle. The blood test wasn't completed, but I knew what it would show. The doctor was right. Denying the facts wouldn't change anything.

My emotions were drained. I felt like I was being punished. I needed help, but who could I talk to? Who could help me?

"God, You're all I have right now. But I thought that when I committed this rape to You, that would be the end of its effect on me." As I spoke to God, I realized how incapable I was of handling this crushing news. Though I had thought my commitment of the situation to Him would solve the problem, I had to admit that perhaps I didn't understand what commitment really was. Maybe the reason I was in this mess was because I was still trying to run my life. I had given Christ a place to live in me, but deep inside I knew that I was still calling the shots. I felt Him pressing in on me, asking for control of my decisions, friendships, time, career, attitudes—everything. And I realized that without Christ in charge there was no hope of my overcoming this problem and succeeding in life.

"Lord, I'm so unhappy with my life," I prayed. "I seem to have no control over the things that happen to me. If You don't help me, Lord, if You don't take control of my life, then there's no hope for me."

I cried again, quietly this time before I continued my prayer. "God, how much more can I take? Please help me. Take my life. I have nothing left. I surrender it totally to You. I'm looking to You for guidance. I'm not asking You to make my life rosy. Just help me get through this mess. I'll accept the results, whatever they are, but I can't go on without You in control."

Finally I was able to drive home. Mom was still at work and my sisters were in school. I grabbed my Bible. Overcome by my emotions, I was desperate to hear some words from God. But where would I find the hope I so desperately needed? I was still relatively unfamiliar with this Book. I picked up the correspondence course and saw a passage in the book of Proverbs. I had to look in the table of contents to find it, then I read these words:

Trust in the Lord with all your heart,
    and do not lean on your own understanding.
In all your ways acknowledge Him,
    and He will make your paths straight.[4]

I clung to those words. God *was* helping me. Here was a promise I could lean on. In my car I had made the first step by surrendering control of my life. Now God had shown me the next step. I would express my trust by acknowledging Him in all my ways. I would wait to hear from the Lord what I should do next.

But first I had to rest. As I lay down on my bed I realized that I had to tell my mother the news, even though I already knew what her reaction would be: She would not be able to handle it. How would she explain it to my sisters? She had too many hurts of her own to even begin to try to help me. Still, no matter what her response, I would have to tell her.

What then? The only other person I could talk to

was Zoe. But what could she do? I needed someplace to go. But where? This was like trying to put together a complex puzzle. And I wasn't even sure I had all the pieces.

Did God? I had that promise from Proverbs. It was time to trust that He did have the pieces and to let Him decide how they would all fit together.

4

Displaced Person

I waited to tell my mother until I received confirmation of my condition. The expected news came two days later at work, when a nurse called to tell me that the pregnancy blood test was positive. There was no doubt about my condition. That evening while Kay and Sue were playing outside and Mom was in the kitchen fixing dinner, I took a deep breath and raised my voice to get her attention. "Mother, I got the test results from the doctor today," I stammered.

"And?" she said without looking up from the stove.

"It's not the flu. I'm pregnant."

With that last word she froze. Then she turned and glared at me with a look of disbelief and slowly shook her head. "No!" she said. "No! Good God, Lee, how could you do this to me? This is too much. I can't handle it. We've just moved into this neighborhood and we're trying to make a new start. What will the neighbors think? You'll have to leave. I can't have your sisters seeing this. How could you do this to them? No, you'll have to get out. You'll have to take care of this yourself . . ."

Mom's tirade was interrupted when the front door opened and my sisters came running into the apartment. I could tell from Mom's expression that there was nothing more to be said. She didn't want an explanation from me; she simply wanted the problem to disappear, which meant I had to leave. We could argue, we could fight, I could cry, but nothing would change the fact that I would have to deal with my problem alone. I wasn't going to receive any support from her.

I was disappointed but not crushed, for I really couldn't expect her to say, "Lee, I'm so sorry. Tell me how it happened." I wanted to explain the circumstances, to have her understand, for if my own mother wouldn't support me, who would? Yet I had to realize that it was all she could do just to get out of bed each morning and face her job and take care of three kids. If I left home, she could deny this had ever happened, and someday I could return with pride, as long as it was *without* the baby.

The next evening I participated in a USO function near San Jose. On the bus with several other girls, I heard one of them mention the word "abortion." Casually I entered the conversation, saying, "I've never known anyone who actually *had* an abortion."

Judy responded, "They're hard to get. I have a friend who got one in Tijuana. It was expensive, but it did solve her problem."

"What exactly do they do?" someone asked.

"It's a relatively simple operation. They go in, remove the fetus, then sew you back up. My friend had no problems."

"Sounds ugly," one of the girls remarked, then changed the subject.

I sensed that if I wanted it, Judy could provide more information. Considering the circumstances, I felt justified in considering this alternative. But I was also uneasy. It sounded like something bad girls did. More important, Judy's description made me realize that there was a baby *alive* inside me. It seemed that abortion was such a permanent answer to a temporary problem.

I knew enough to know that one of God's commandments was "Thou shalt not kill." If I was really serious about letting God run my life, then this wasn't an option. But I could understand why a woman would be tempted to opt for this apparently "easy out."

While the other girls chattered, I thought again about my options. Didn't the Catholics have a home for unwed mothers? What about adoption? Should I keep the baby or let another family have it? Should I stay in San Francisco or move to another area, where my mother and sisters wouldn't have to face me?

It was too much to sort through. As we arrived at an Army base, I tried to put it out of my mind and have a good time. I wasn't very successful.

The next day at work I phoned Zoe and invited myself over for dinner. That night as we were cleaning up the dinner dishes, I broke the news. "Zoe, I've got a problem. I just found out I'm pregnant."

There was a look of shock on her face, but without condemnation. She quickly reached for a hand towel, dried her hands, and said, "Come, let's sit down."

Zoe was not only my oldest sister but a loyal friend who would hear my problem and try to help. She asked some necessary questions without prying. "I tried to talk to Mom," I explained, "but she can't handle this."

"Are you planning to get married?"

"No, that's out of the question. It was a guy at work that I hope I never see again."

Zoe didn't press me for more details. "Okay, where do we go from here?"

"I don't know. I think what I need to do is to leave town so I won't see this guy again. It would be great if I found someplace where I could go until this whole thing's over. A place where someone understands, like you—only not you because you've got your own kids to take care of. I need someplace where I can think things through. I'll need to get a job and a car of my own."

"Are you going to give the baby up for adoption?"

"I don't know. I'm not in a very good position to raise a child. But I'm not really ready to decide. I need some time to sort things out."

"I think you're right about getting out of town. Every

time you see Mom she'll be reminded of your problem.
You could take my car. I know it's old, but it will probably
do until you can get something better. But where can
you go?"

Zoe thought for a moment about some of the friends
and family she knew on her husband's side. We were
raised without any knowledge of or contact with relatives
such as grandparents, uncles, or cousins. Both Mom and
Dad were only children. But Zoe's husband had some
natural and adopted relatives. "My husband has an old
adopted uncle who lives at the beach. He's blind, and I
think he lives alone. Let me give him a call."

She made the call while I started washing the dishes.
In a few minutes she was back. "It's all set. He has a big
old house and he says there's no problem with you using
one of the bedrooms. I think it's just what we're looking
for."

"Where exactly does he live?" I asked.

"Right between Los Angeles and Long Beach. It's
a long drive, but you can make it in a day."

That night I packed my bags. It didn't take long; I
simply didn't have that many possessions. Sue wanted
to know what I was doing. "I'm moving to Los Angeles,"
I replied.

"Wow! What are you going to do there?"

"I'm getting a new job," I answered confidently.

"Are you going to be a Hollywood star?" she teased,
making an exaggerated Marilyn Monroe pose.

I laughed and tossed a pillow at her. Sue went running to tell Kay the news.

The next morning I informed my surprised boss that
this was my last day of work. Jack had not made an
appearance since that fateful night, and I was glad to
escape before he had the chance. After work I tossed my
belongings in Zoe's car and said goodbye to my family.
Sue and Kay said they would come and visit me when I
became rich and famous. Mom just said, "God bless you.
You take care."

I swung by Zoe's to say goodbye to her and her

family. She stuffed 50 dollars into my purse to go with the approximately 50 dollars that represented my entire savings. Then, with an hour of sunlight left and a road map spread out on the front seat, I was on Highway 101 heading south. It didn't take many miles before the intense loneliness hit me. I was going to a city where I knew no one. In fact, I felt vaguely uneasy about the living situation that had been arranged for me. I tossed that anxiety aside, since I really had no alternative, and thought of the other questions: Where will I find a job? How quickly can I buy a car so Zoe can have hers back? Will I make new friends easily? Will I keep the baby? How does one give a baby up for adoption?

"Wait!" I told myself. "Let's just worry about one problem at a time. Right now you have a place to live. What you need is a job. That's enough to think about. Take one day at a time."

With that I tried to relax as I moved down the coast. But my mind wouldn't relax. It jumped from emotion to emotion. There was relief in leaving home, but fear about the future; there was a sense of adventure, but also resentment at being forced to uproot. And deep within me there was something—a deep emotion I couldn't yet express—that needed to escape. Sometime after midnight I concluded that there was no reason to rush to my destination, so I checked into a seedy "No-Tell Motel" joint just off the highway.

In my tawdry room I stretched out on the bed and stared at the ugly flowered bedspread. Despair surfaced and drained my strength. I felt empty, deserted, and isolated. There was no one to support me, no one to confide in—except God. It seemed logical to talk to Him aloud, as if He were my friend sitting in the chair opposite my bed. I didn't try to make my prayer sound holy. I just expressed my thoughts and feelings as they surfaced.

"Lord, my life's a mess. It was a mess before I handed it over to You, and it's still a mess. Nothing's changed. I don't expect You to be a divine slot machine where I drop in the prayer and You spit out a blessing, but God, I sure could use a jackpot right now. I have no family, no home, and practically no money.

"Is this Your idea of punishing me? Maybe I was wrong to tear my family away from my father. But how was I to know? It seemed like the right thing to do at the time. Well, at least I won't be a burden to my mother anymore. It was good to get away from her so she won't be embarrassed. Now I've just got to rely on You to help me get this thing over with and behind me."

As I talked to God I felt anger surge from deep within, and my words reflected it. "Look, God, You could have prevented this. Why did You let me open my stupid mouth at the office! Why did You allow that man to invite me to his home? Why didn't one of the other girls come too? None of this makes any sense.

"And now I feel robbed. I saved my virginity for this? Do You realize I'm only 18 years old? I'm too young for all this responsibility. I never had a chance to just be a kid. How come? Why couldn't I have enjoyed life for a while?"

I rambled on for nearly an hour venting my frustration. When I was done my arm, seemingly on its own, reached for the Gideon Bible in the drawer of the nightstand. Without my correspondence course I didn't know where to turn. I lost my grip as I thumbed through the pages, and it flopped open on my lap. My eyes fell on the words of Jesus teaching His disciples to pray:

After this manner therefore pray ye:

Our Father which art in heaven,
Hallowed be thy name.
Thy kingdom come.
Thy will be done in earth, as it is in heaven.
Give us this day our daily bread.
And forgive us our debts, as we forgive our
    debtors . . .[1]

As I continued reading, I saw that Christ explained the importance of forgiveness: "For if ye forgive men their trespasses, your heavenly Father will also forgive you; but if ye forgive not men their trespasses, neither will your Father forgive your trespasses."[2]

Suddenly I realized that this applied to me!

That scared me. What happens if I'm not forgiven? I couldn't live with that uncertainty. I needed to make sure that I had fulfilled God's requirement. I needed to forgive those who had hurt me. This wasn't optional. God made it very clear—either/or, black or white. The only question was whether I would obey Him.

Really I had no choice. Given the facts and my circumstances, this was my only hope. I had to obey. It didn't matter whether I felt like it or not. I had surrendered control of my life to Christ, and I wanted to experience His love and forgiveness. For the next few hours I reviewed my life and, continuing to talk out loud, expressed to God my forgiveness for the many people who had hurt me.

It was natural to think first of my mother, and how she would not support me in my trauma and had put me out of my home. But much as it hurt, it was relatively easy to forgive her, for what else could she do? She simply couldn't handle any more. In less than a year her marriage had ended and she had moved 3000 miles away from the small section of Philadelphia that was the only home she had ever known. After all the pain she had endured from my father, I could understand why she couldn't face any more humiliation from me.

I reflected back on my life in Philadelphia. I thought of my father and how he would begin each day not with the Breakfast of Champions but with a raw egg in a glass of gin. He rarely ate a meal with the family, and in fact his dexterity with a fork was witnessed only during the holidays. "Lord, I want to forgive my father for the embarrassment he caused me," I said. "I forgive him for all the beatings and for his lack of care. I forgive him for not being there when I needed him, for not reaching out when I was hurting, for getting drunk and embarrassing me so many times in front of my friends or the neighbors, for being a loser who couldn't provide for his family."

As I spoke those words, I began to cry, for in the midst of my confession I began to see my father in a new light. The man I saw as my father was not the real person. In some way that I didn't really understand, he was sick. It was the booze that had changed him. Underneath was a man who wanted to love his daughters, but his thinking had become distorted. Because of the alcohol, he couldn't control himself. He had never dealt with the resentments of his past, and as unresolved anger had built up within him, his drinking had increased to compensate, which only exaggerated the change in his personality.

My parents weren't the only ones I needed to forgive, for I had stored up all kinds of small wounds for years. I thought of teachers who had embarrassed me or put me down, friends who had rejected me, a boyfriend who had abruptly ended a relationship I thought had potential, and the drama teacher who hadn't picked me for a choice part in a musical I had tried out for. As I recalled each individual hurt, I forgave the person responsible for that hurt.

And then I thought of my attacker—the one who had disrupted my life, who was forcing me to flee from my family, who had robbed me of my youth. How could I possibly forgive him? I didn't want to, yet I had to. "If ye forgive not men their trespasses, neither will your Father forgive your trespasses." Was I going to obey God? He offered me a promise—if I followed His instructions.

When I hesitated, I thought of Jesus Christ and how He had wrestled with God's plan on the night before He was crucified. He prayed in agony, "If it be possible, let this cup pass from me; nevertheless not as I will, but as thou wilt."[3] And while He was hanging on the cross He said, "My God, my God, why hast thou forsaken me?"[4]

Jesus was a victim too, one who hadn't done anything wrong at all. But despite His personal emotions, He obeyed His Father.

That's how I felt: victimized. Apart from an error in judgment, I hadn't done anything wrong. But that wasn't the issue. The question was "Will you forgive that man?" I thought about why he might have done it. Did he really intend to ruin my life, to make me pregnant, to force me to quit my job and move 400 miles away from my family? It seemed to me that he had planned to catch me alone, but that he probably didn't know the ramifications of his actions. I had to forgive him for what he had done, not for what he intended. "Lord, I forgive him. I can't judge his thoughts. But his actions have hurt me deeply and altered the course of my life. I forgive him not because I feel like it but because You have told me to do so."

That was the hardest, but I wasn't finished, for I still felt resentment and anger toward God. I needed to forgive Him, too. Not for doing wrong to me—He can never sin. But there were options in His sovereign wisdom that He chose not to exercise. He did not prevent the rape or the pregnancy. He didn't warn me so that I could have avoided the danger. He didn't intervene in any way. I felt as though He had just left me alone. If I was going to hold those things against Him, then I was cutting myself off from Him, and He was all I had right now.

"Lord, I admit I was wrong for holding You responsible for my circumstances. You never promised that I would be free from pain. I realize that I've been angry at You for not coming to my rescue, for not preventing this. I want to hold tight to You from now on."

Finally, I had to forgive myself. For being so naive and trusting. For not making the right choices. For not living up to my Doris Day fantasy. For not being able to pull all the strings of my life and make everything turn out nice. For not "making it" like I thought everyone should "make it." I had to realize that it was okay to be me as God created me, and to acknowledge that I needed God's help.

The early dawn light was starting to creep into my dingy motel room. I had talked aloud with God for several hours, and I now felt a marvelous new freedom within. My intense anger and resentment was being defused by my confession to God and His forgiveness. The guilt of my sins was being lifted. The alienation I had so keenly felt toward my family had now disappeared. I was free from my anger and desire for retaliation. The obstacles between me and God, that I hadn't even realized were there, were fading away.

It felt like my old life had just been washed away, and a new life had begun. How ironic, I thought, that the life growing inside me was actually the agent bringing me to a birth of my spiritual walk with God! Now I realized how little I had experienced of Christ. I had given Him only a tiny part of my life in Philadelphia, and a little more a few days ago in the car after I learned I was pregnant.

Now I was beginning to experience a much deeper relationship with Him. He was real, as real as if He were actually physically sitting in that chair by my bed as I talked to Him. There was a sense of hope that God was taking this ugly situation and turning it into something that would bring me closer to Him.

"Lord, I don't want to lose this sense of Your presence. I feel this is a new start. I know now that You're real, and I want to hold tightly to You. I don't have a husband, or a mother or father, or even a good friend right now. Lord, You'll have to take their place. You be my husband, my father, my mother, my friend."

As the light began to grow brighter outside, I decided to try to sleep for a couple of hours before resuming my journey. My perspective had changed so much in this tiny motel room. Last night at dusk my life had looked so bleak. Now, as the sun was rising, I had a sense of warmth that caused me to view the future with a sense of adventure. Look what had already happened in one night! Sure, there were many uncertainties. But now I knew I was not traveling alone. As I drifted off to sleep I thought, "Lee, you've got to stay plugged into this." And I wondered, "Can this really last, or am I just experiencing a catharsis that will wear off in a couple of days?"

5

Finding My Way

There was a sense of adventure as I crested the hills above Los Angeles and headed down into the smog. So this was the home of the Beach Boys! Well, they sure weren't singing about a pregnant "little surfer girl." But for someone from the inner city of Philadelphia, the palm trees, white sandy beaches, and freeways filled me with plenty of excitement.

From my human viewpoint, the future was filled with uncertainty. But I was very aware that I was not traveling alone. The warmth of my encounter with God in the motel room had remained just as real when I awoke from my two-hour nap, and even now continued with me. "Just the essentials, Lord," I prayed. "I don't need any luxuries. Just food and shelter. Your love has already been extravagant!" How comforting it was to know that I could talk with the Lord and include Him in all my rambling thoughts!

As I passed through downtown Los Angeles, it occurred to me that I had to keep this relationship going, but I wasn't sure how to. "I've got to find some other people who feel this same life," I thought to myself and God. "It would help a lot in the coming months if I had some support from people who share this same relationship with Christ." I determined that as soon as I settled into my new home, I would find a church.

It didn't take long to find Uncle Howard's home. It was an old gray-and-blue two-story house just off the beach. It must have been built in the 1920's, for it looked a little like an old ship: porthole windows, smokestack chimney, and second-story deck!

I knocked on the front door, but no one answered. Hesitantly I tried the handle and the door opened. A horrible musty smell greeted me, as if this home had been shut up tight for years. Two 70-year-old-plus men were inside, smoking cigars and watching TV in over-stuffed chairs. One was Uncle Howard and the other was an older brother who was obviously in poor health. I quickly learned that both lived there, and they were glad to see me. Whether I liked it or not, they obviously expected me to become their housekeeper, do the laundry, cook, and take care of them. Doris Day was really out this time. I would be more like Hazel the maid.

However, there wasn't much choice. The place obviously hadn't been cleaned for years. Ashtrays overflowing with cigar ashes littered the disheveled living room. When I looked in the kitchen for something to eat, I saw dirty dishes piled up on the counter and old food and garbage that had attracted an army of ants. I couldn't even think of eating in such a mess. They didn't seem to mind how dirty the house was, but I did. I dropped my bags in the extra room upstairs and instantly began a quick cleanup campaign. It took nearly all my energy to pry open a couple of windows. That action plus dusting, throwing out the garbage, and emptying all the ashtrays helped clear some of the stale air.

I was surprised to discover that Uncle Howard wasn't totally blind. He saw enough to move easily around the house, find things in the kitchen, watch television, and even walk across the street. His vision was impaired, but he seemed to relish the pity he received because his family thought he was blind.

My apprehensions about this living situation had proved valid, but what could I do? Here was my first test for trusting God. Every night I spent time reading the Bible, and I found an answer in Philippians: "Whatsoever things are true, whatsoever things are honest, whatsoever things are just, whatsoever things are pure, whatsoever things are lovely, whatsoever things are of good report; if there be any virtue, and if there be any praise, *think on these things.*"[1] I could choose to look at this crummy situation and say, "I'm getting out of here —pronto." Or I could thank God for what He had provided for me right now and recognize that I could serve God by helping these two old men. I decided to do the latter and make the best of the situation. At least I had a room of my own, which was something I had never enjoyed before.

It took less than a week to find a job as a secretary in an old beachfront hotel. Then I began looking for a church. I didn't see any of the beautiful old Gothic structures like the ones I had attended in Philadelphia. "California-style" churches looked streamlined and modern. On the first Sunday I visited a church just a few blocks away. The service seemed to emphasize social activities and political causes, without any mention of the Bible. I knew this wasn't what I needed. The next week I visited a religious science church because it had a cross on its building. I never heard Jesus mentioned once throughout the service.

Those two experiences showed me what I needed in a church. It had to teach the Bible, and it had to honor Jesus Christ. So I looked in the Yellow Pages and couldn't believe all the denominations listed! Just under Baptist alone there were at least half a dozen different kinds of churches. Under one listing for a Baptist church I found the phrase "Where the Bible is Taught." I decided that this was where I would make my next visit.

The church was a large building that was less than half full. Perhaps 300 people attended, listening to a dull preacher—nothing at all like Billy Graham. However, he talked about Jesus and preached from the Bible. And, just like Billy Graham, he invited people to come forward and receive Jesus. That was good enough for me.

After the service a great big woman with an equally big smile greeted me and said, "Where are you going for lunch, girl?" That was my introduction to Villa (Mom) Croft. I followed her and her short, skinny husband ("B.B.") to a tiny house just half a block from the church. "Let's see what we've got in the refrigerator," she said as she began digging out eggs and other assorted food.

"Just moved here, didn't you?" she said as she started cooking eggs, grits, and biscuits.

"Yes, how did you know?"

"I can tell," she said with a twinkle in her eye. "Mom Croft can spot a lonely, hungry girl. Now you just relax and make yourself at home. We may not have much, but we love sharing what we have. Wasn't that a good sermon this morning? We can never spend too much time in the Bible. No, ma'am. Carol, come over here and meet Lee."

Carol was the Croft's 30-year-old daughter, and she had just come into the house with her two small boys. "Carol's living with us right now," Mom said after introductions. "Aren't those two of the cutest kids you've ever seen? It's a shame their daddy left them. He just up and walked out one day. They had no place to go, so of course we told them to move right in . . ."

Mom kept right on talking to me like I was a long-time member of the family. There wasn't much room around the small kitchen table, but we all squeezed in and everyone had plenty to eat. From the way I was included, I sensed that I wasn't the first "stray" they had invited to dinner. I couldn't believe the love I felt from Mom and Dad Croft. Obviously they sacrificed for their daughter and her two sons, but, as with the food, there was more than enough love to go around. How ironic that I had seen so many people who tried to hold onto whatever love and acceptance they had; this couple not only had enough for themselves, but they could give it away! I had never seen a family quite like this before.

"Why don't you come back tonight and visit our singles group?" Carol suggested after lunch.

"Singles group?" I asked.

She laughed as she described it. "Well, we're not much. A bunch of old maids and a couple of pitiful fellows. But we have a good time. We study the Bible and kind of bolster one another."

So I started going to church Sundays and Wednesday nights, and participated in the singles group. I was glad I didn't look pregnant yet, so it was easy to fit in. But these young adults hadn't had a new convert in their midst for some time, and they weren't prepared for my "unbaptist" ideas. At one early meeting we were talking about the lack of money in the singles fund, so I raised my hand and made a suggestion. "Why don't we put on a square dance in the fellowship hall? We can bring in straw and have everyone dress up in Western clothes . . ."

The stunned look on the faces of the group made me stop in midsentence. They obviously didn't agree that this was a brainstorm from God. Carol saved the day. She stood up, put her arm around me, and said, "Now, guys, Lee doesn't know all the rules and regulations around here." As I sat down she whispered, "We'll have to shelve that idea for now. Maybe we can do it another time."

I was baffled. I didn't know *anybody* who didn't dance. And these looked like such happy, well-adjusted people. I guess I had a lot to learn.

The group began to find my observations about the Scriptures amusing as well as occasionally challenging and insightful. A gray-haired old man led the Sunday school lesson from a dry old leader's guide. It seemed like everyone had heard this stuff for years. But it was all new to me. Everything seemed to apply directly to me, and I treated it as spiritual food helping me prepare for the ordeal ahead. The group laughed and tolerated my enthusiasm, for I didn't have a "fundamentalist" slant on anything.

One Sunday we were talking about Jesus and His

disciples, and reference was made to the mother of James and John, who asked Jesus to place her sons on His right and left hand. Immediately I thought of the Jewish mothers I had known in Philadelphia. "Can't you see a big, pushy Jewish mother barging through the crowd?" I told the group when we were invited to share our comments. "She's saying, 'So who's going to sit on your right hand and left? Such nice boys—you shouldn't pass them up.' James and John must have been embarrassed to death."

The class laughed at my "authentic" Jewish accent. But I wasn't doing it to tell a joke. I went on to make this point: "Wasn't that something—this mother telling God what to do? But don't we do the same thing? I know I do. I want to tell the Lord what to do."

"You're right," the teacher answered. "I've never thought of it quite like that before. That's a good application."

Lunch with the Crofts after Sunday morning service became a routine for me. I was beginning to bulge slightly in front, but I don't think any of them noticed. Or if they did, they probably figured it was because of their good food. I hadn't told anyone that I was pregnant, but I knew I couldn't hide the obvious much longer.

It was surprisingly easy to tell Mom and Carol Croft my secret. My first reaction to the rape and pregnancy had been normal: "Where did I go wrong?" I had also had a desperate urge to hide my shame. Now for the first time I was experiencing unconditional love, and I felt safe. I was beginning to see myself in a new light. I was not a loser, responsible for and deserving of every bad experience. One Sunday after dinner I blurted out to Mom and Carol that I was pregnant. Much to my relief, it didn't seem to faze them in the least. Carol agreed, at Mom Croft's suggestion, to communicate it to the singles group during a time when I wasn't there, so that they wouldn't be shocked.

That experience showed me how much I could trust this dear family. It was as if God was giving me a mother and sister to replace the family I had lost. I now felt an increasing desire to tell someone about the rape, and I felt I could trust Carol with this secret. One evening I gathered all my courage and told her the circumstances of how I'd been raped. She was obviously horrified, yet she seemed to understand and sympathize. Her anger was directed not at me but at the injustice of the situation. "Did you report it to the police?" she asked.

"No, I didn't see any sense in it," I admitted, embarrassed.

"Why not? That creep should have been prosecuted."

"But I thought it was only against the law if the girl was 17 years old or less."

"Where did you get that idea? Rape is a felony. If you didn't report it, that man can go and hurt someone else."

"I also was afraid for my mother. She couldn't have handled the embarrassment."

"You never gave her the chance," Carol said. "Well," she continued, slowing down, "you should have reported it. But should have's don't count now. It's water over the dam. The fact is that you're here now" she comforted as she took my hand "and we're going to help you get through this."

Carol told her mother this information, and she was also most understanding. "You know, Honey, God works His purpose through all these situations in our lives. You don't know what this will lead to."

I was coming to a similar conclusion from my own study of the Bible. Every day I spent an hour or more reading and meditating on the Bible. It was like a salve to my damaged emotions, and it kept the fire of my renewed relationship with God burning bright.

One of the recurring themes I found was that of thankfulness:

> In everything *give thanks*, for this is God's will for you. . . .[2]

Whatever you do in word or deed, do all in the name of the Lord Jesus, *giving thanks* through Him to God the Father.[3]

Be anxious for nothing, but in everything by prayer and supplication *with thanksgiving* let your requests be made known to God.[4]

After being jarred repeatedly by that message, I realized I needed to practice thanksgiving. This didn't mean I had to be resigned to my situation, but it meant that I needed to focus on the good things God was doing and to trust Him to bring me through the negative things that remained in my life. And so I practiced being thankful: "Thank You, Lord, for giving me a place to live. Thank You for a church where I can learn more about You. Thank You for a singles group that accepts me. Thank You for Mom and Dad Croft and Carol, who love me as if I were a member of their family. Thank You for the friend at church who loaned me a car so Zoe could have hers back. Thank You for a good job that gives me enough money to meet my needs."

I didn't find any Scripture that said sorrow and hardship would be eliminated from my life, but I found promises that assured me God was with me in my trials. I clung to the promises the apostle Paul wrote:

If God is for us, who is against us? . . . Who shall separate us from the love of Christ? Shall tribulation, or distress, or persecution, or famine, or nakedness, or peril, or sword? . . . But in all these things we overwhelmingly conquer through Him who loved us. For I am convinced that neither death, nor life, nor angels, nor principalities, nor things present, nor things to come, nor powers, nor height, nor depth, nor any other created thing, shall be able to separate us from the love of God, which is in Christ Jesus our Lord.[5]

This convinced me that nothing resulting from my assault had to come between me and the love of Christ. It was another reason to be thankful, for I saw how this experience was truly drawing me closer to God. Then I saw God's love demonstrated again in a potentially devastating situation.

It happened late one evening as I was falling asleep at the "odd fellows' " home. Suddenly Uncle Howard burst into my room. "What's the matter?" I yelled. He didn't answer but started approaching my bed with obviously one thing on his mind. I jumped up and pushed the bed between us. "Stop it, you dirty old man!"

"I'm not going to hurt you!" he sneered as he climbed on the bed and prepared to jump on me.

"Get away from me!" I screamed. I scrambled around the bed and dashed out the door and down the stairs. Uncle Howard's brother heard the commotion and came out to see what was going on. That gave me time to phone Mom Croft. "It's Lee. Quick, please come over and get me. I'm in trouble!"

The two old men were arguing now, so I quickly threw my belongings into some shopping bags. Within five minutes Mom Croft burst into the house like Wonder Woman, dressed only in her nightgown and a robe. The fire in her eyes immediately silenced Uncle Howard, who backed up the stairs. "Let's go, Honey!" She grabbed three of my bags, took me by the arm, and led me right to her car.

As we drove to her home Mom said, "Now you don't worry about a thing. Mom Croft's going to take care of you. We'll fix you a place to sleep at the house, and you just stay with us until you have your baby."

From her manner, I knew this wasn't open for discussion. She meant exactly what she said. God didn't have to tell me to be thankful in this situation. It came very naturally. It had never been more obvious that He was looking out for me.

6

Shelter of Love

The Crofts were modern-day Good Samaritans. They really didn't have room for me in their home, but they made room anyway. Every available space was used for bedrooms. I shared a room with Carol's two little boys. This house had nothing fancy—no little knick-knacks, but just the essentials. Dad Croft, who was nearing retirement age, worked nearby for Hughes Aircraft. They weren't poor, but the Crofts put their money into people rather than material possessions. They had the rare gift of generosity, for their world was so big that there was always room for those who were in need or unwanted by others. Many times when we sat down to a meal there would be a stranger at the table with us, and these guests always knew that it was the Crofts' love for Christ that compelled them to minister in this way.

Here I was at peace for the first time in many months. Here I was in a refuge from strife and disharmony; there would be no more unexpected and shocking attacks. But I was also learning not to put my hope in this family or any human situation. It wasn't a cynical spirit, in which I was afraid something would go wrong, but rather a realization that God was taking care of me now, and that I could go on trusting Him to wonderfully provide for me.

It was becoming more obvious all the time that the

baby was growing inside me. But with that growth there was also a love for Christ growing. Since that night of prayer in the Central California motel, my desire to know Christ and do His will had flourished. I felt His love producing a contentment in my life that I had never known before. There was also a quiet anticipation as I waited to see God work in my circumstances. Even with the continuing distress of my pregnancy, I had lost all desire to lash out at God. He was definitely turning an ugly situation into something beautiful.

More and more the baby was becoming a real person to me. I began feeling some hopes and expectations for it. Would he or she look like me? What kind of personality and temperament and interests would it have? Would it grow up to love God the way I did? I found myself *wanting* this baby, and wanting the best possible life for it.

One evening I read from Psalm 139: "You made all the delicate, inner parts of my body, and knit them together in my mother's womb. . . . Your workmanship is marvelous. . . . You were there while I was being formed in utter seclusion! You saw me before I was born and scheduled each day of my life before I began to breathe."[1]

Those words powerfully reminded me that this baby was not a mistake. This was not an "illegitimate child." Yes, there had been an illegitimate and illegal act. But the life inside me was now in the hands of God, and there were no illegitimate births when it was God who created life. God made all human life legitimate, regardless of the circumstances surrounding conception.

Soon after I moved in with the Crofts, I assumed a leadership role with the singles group. It was crazy to think of a pregnant singles group leader! Few in the group knew that my pregnancy was the result of a rape, yet they made no judgments about my virtue. Neither did the older Christians at the church pressure me into a confession that might satisfy their curiosity. Instead they demonstrated their love for Christ by loving me, which made me want to live my life all the more for Christ.

I was learning many practical lessons through the church. All of the Bible was coming alive, even the Old Testament. I couldn't seem to get enough of the stories about men and women who had suffered and seen God work. One of the most meaningful stories was that of Joseph. Talk about getting a raw deal! This innocent boy found himself a victim of circumstances over which he absolutely had no control. Because Joseph was the favorite child of his father, Jacob, Joseph's jealous brothers conspired against him and sold him to some passing traders, who transported him into Egypt.

Poor young Joey hardly knew what hit him. He became a slave because of the terrorist actions of his own brothers. How could this have slipped by God? Was God asleep at the time, or on a break? Surely He could not have been involved in this scheme.

But it got worse. Joseph did a great job for his master, and all was going well until his boss's wife accused Joseph of trying to seduce her. For the next several years Joseph languished in prison and sharpened his gift of discerning the meaning of dreams.

Then came the day when Pharaoh needed a disturbing dream interpreted, and Joseph was the only one who could do it. Joseph correctly informed the ruler that Egypt would have seven years of plenty followed by seven years of famine. Joseph recommended that Pharaoh store a portion of his harvest during the first seven years to provide during the famine. Pharaoh was so impressed that he appointed Joseph to oversee the project and made him the second-most-powerful man in the land.

This was precisely where God wanted Joseph to be. So what could I say? God didn't make all this evil happen, but He did allow the circumstances to work into His overall plan.

In order to help me work this out, I pictured God operating His divine computer. A computer can only work as well as the information fed into it. As in Joseph's case, my information was limited, but God had all the facts. He is never shocked or surprised by our problems. He knew how Joseph's problems fit into the total picture, and Joseph was willing to let God coordinate that.

Joseph didn't see the purpose in all his trials until his brothers came begging for grain during the famine, probably 20 or more years after they had sold their brother. This could have been an opportunity for revenge. But instead, Joseph, after revealing himself to his brothers, said, "Do not be grieved or angry with yourselves because you sold me here, *for God sent me* before you to preserve life."[2]

The point for me was that it wasn't God who did this evil deed, but Joseph's brothers. Joseph recognized that fact, but he also realized that God did not intervene and stop it because He was going to use it. "God sent me before you,"[3] Joseph said. He summed it up well after his father died and his brothers were afraid that Joseph would now take revenge:

> You intended to harm me, *but God intended it for good* to accomplish what is now being done. . . .[4]

What an example to follow! Rather than decipher who was to blame for my circumstances, I needed to recognize that God had a plan. *There was a purpose in my pain.* Though my attacker meant evil toward me, somehow God would use it for good. When I was able to honestly accept that my present set of circumstances were good, even though there was evil in the process of getting there, I was able to relax. God was turning the evil done to me into good.

I read another Old Testament verse that confirmed this truth:

"I know the plans I have for you," declares the
Lord, "plans to prosper you and not to harm
you, plans to give you hope and a future."[5]

I had to believe this promise even if I never saw or
understood the full picture of what God was doing.

So what was my response? Earlier I had questioned
God and asked, "Why me?" God had answered, "Why
not you?" and I had realized that no one was exempt
from problems. Now my question was, "Lord, do You
trust me with this?" This was not an accident, something
that had slipped past His desk. He had decided that He
could *trust* me with this problem. When the request had
passed over His desk, He had stamped "yes" on it. He
didn't expect me to handle it alone. He was with me.

I decided that if God felt He could trust me with
this pregnancy, then I needed to believe it would all
work into His plan for my life, for my benefit rather than
my destruction. I would assume that this predicament
was custom-designed by the Great Carpenter to bring
me closer to maturity. I needed to consider myself a
trustee rather than a victim, and trust God with the
outcome.

One Sunday morning the pastor used two sermon
illustrations to explain what it meant to trust God. The
first was a story about a man who was working on his
roof when he slipped and wound up hanging onto the
gutter by his fingertips as he dangled 20 feet above the
ground. He cried out, "God, is there anybody up there
who can help me?" A voice from heaven boomed back,
"Trust in Me and let go." The man considered that for
a moment, then cried out again, "Is there anybody else
up there who can help?"

The pastor made the point that we have a tendency
to cling to things and refuse to "let go and let God." Yet
by clinging to those things, we are held captive. He
illustrated with a second example about how monkeys
are captured in the forest. Knowing their curiosity, the
would-be captors hollow out a coconut and place a special

monkey treat inside it. Later a monkey will stick his hand inside to retrieve the treat, but finds he cannot pull his fist back out through the hole without releasing the goody. Inevitably he refuses to let go and is captured.

Those two illustrations and the story of Joseph helped me see that I had to release my hold on my life—including my broken dreams of the past and my hopes for the future—and let my dreams and expectations be centered in God. As I did so, I felt a new freedom, as if God had added yet another piece of the puzzle in the process of answering my questions.

I was seven months pregnant during the Christmas season as I participated in the singing of Handel's "Messiah." I found that the rich music had a new meaning for me. As the tenor soloist sang "And the crooked shall be made straight, and the rough places plain," I smiled because I felt it was happening in my life. When the chorus sang "He shall feed His flock like a shepherd and gather the lambs in his arms, and carry them in his bosom, and shall gently lead those that are with young," it gave me a warm glow, for I sensed that the Shepherd was doing exactly that for me. It almost seemed strange, but it was true: In the midst of a situation that I knew could have been devastating, God really was giving me His peace.

Another significant moment came right after the New Year. I had seen several baptism services at the church and couldn't believe they actually put people under the water instead of just sprinkling them. I attended the baptism classes and learned that this was a clear instruction of the Bible. Since the Bible was now my standard, I decided to take the step. Eight months pregnant, this singles group leader made a public statement, through baptism, that my old life was washed away and that I now had a new life with Christ. It was also a time to publicly renew my commitment to God.

The lessons I was learning in church and the evidence of God's love in the Croft home made me realize how much I wanted to have my child raised in a Christian environment. It also made me realize that I could not provide the kind of home the baby needed; it needed to be raised by a caring mother and father. I could not even provide the most basic necessities of a home. As I prayed, I realized that my only alternative was to put the child up for adoption.

It took a lot of phone calls to locate the county adoption agency, which was hidden in the corner of another larger agency. The adoption process involved several visits, numerous forms to fill out, and interviews with a social worker. As I began the process of working with the government agency, I wondered if there would be any problems with my request that the child be raised in a Christian home. But I dismissed that concern, assuming that the agency would automatically honor my desires.

7

The Natural and the Supernatural

There was a peculiar tension at the adoption agency, and it never let up during the hours I spent there on each visit. Part of it was the proximity to the Watts area and part of it was the fact that it was nestled in the midst of several social agencies. The old building, cramped facilities, and run-down furniture seemed designed to communicate the idea that anyone who came in here was a loser.

In the large waiting room we took a number and sat on broken-down vinyl couches. When our number was called we were assigned to a social worker, who handed us forms to fill out. Then we were sentenced to sit for another hour or two until she was ready to see us again. The woman assigned to my case was a large, authoritarian woman with a distinct Southern accent. She carried a military bearing, as if she were a colonel in the service. Her scowl seemed to say, "No fooling around here. No exceptions. You don't give me any problems and I'll get you through this as quickly as possible."

It was easy to feel like I was nothing more than raw material to be processed along an assembly line. Yet I felt different from the other women in the room. Others might consider me a loser, but I didn't. A few months earlier I would have felt intimidated, but now I felt a confident acceptance of this baffling situation. There was a genuine peace that came from the Lord as I worked through the frustrating maze of county processing.

Some of the forms were easy to fill out while others were impossible. One form asked for detailed family background of both the mother and the father, family race and nationalities, birthplaces, addresses, brothers and sisters, education, artistic and athletic talents, medical history, career experiences, military records, and on and on. All of this would supposedly help the agency place the child in the right home. It was all multiple-choice—mark the appropriate boxes. "We're on computer now," the caseworker proudly announced. I didn't understand what a computer's capabilities were, but wondered how this archaic agency could operate one.

On the father's side of the forms, I had nothing to offer but his name. Surprisingly, this didn't seem to concern the social worker too much. Perhaps his name was deposited into the mysterious computer system, where a large amount of information on this man was stored. If so, none of that information was shared with me.

On my side, I made no mention of my father's alcoholism. I didn't know what my child would learn about me later, so why put anything down that might cause unnecessary grief?

There was a section on one of the forms that allowed me to express religious preference. The choices were Catholic, Protestant, Jewish, or none. When I had my first interview with the colonel, she had scanned the form to make sure all the boxes were filled in, and had said, "You didn't check what faith you want your baby raised." She handed me the form and pointed to the choices. "You want Catholic, Protestant, Jewish, or no preference?" she drawled.

"I want a Bible-believing Protestant to raise my baby," I answered.

Instantly I knew from her glare that I was in hot

water. "There ain't no box like that, girl. You got your choices. Now don't give me a hard time."

This was a true test of wills. At the moment, this "wanted" baby was in my charge, and I believed that God wanted me to do everything I could to see that it was properly cared for. Since the only loving and committed people I had encountered were in my Bible-believing church, it was only natural that I put a big "X" in the box marked "Protestant." Then on the bottom of the form I wrote, "Preferably Baptist or Bible-believing home" and drew a big arrow from the box to my answer.

The woman raised her eyebrows at me to demonstrate her exasperation as she reviewed the form. This was more precision than her system could tolerate. I wondered if she thought I was trying to test her, or that I was being arrogant and combative. Maybe she would give me some vague promise to pass the request on, knowing that it wouldn't do any good. "You can't put anything extra here," she announced. "We're on computer now. Scratch this 'preferably' stuff out. You gotta check one or the other of these boxes."

"In that case, I'm not signing the form. I cannot put this baby up for grabs. I'm going to do everything I can."

She glared at me for a moment, then slammed her case-file shut. "We'll talk about this next time." Then mumbling under her breath, she handed me a card noting my next appointment and dismissed me.

In the intervening days I thought a lot about that confrontation. I thought of how Pontius Pilate had tried to impress Jesus with his authority, a little like that social worker had tried to intimidate me. Jesus had answered, "You would have no authority over Me unless it had been given you from above."[1] Jesus was not being belligerent but was simply stating a fact. I was encouraged that this woman didn't have the power to dictate where the baby went.

But what exactly was my reponsibility?

For the answer I reread the story of Moses, which

we had discussed in Sunday school a few weeks earlier. The book of Exodus begins with a description of the children of Israel being held in slavery in Egypt. The more the Egyptians abused the Israelites, the more they multiplied. To reduce the population explosion, the king of Egypt ordered that all newborn Israelite male babies be thrown into the Nile River, something the Egyptians did to their own less-than-perfect babies.

In this setting a woman named Jochebed became pregnant, a rather undesirable state at the time. She gave birth to a son and managed to hide him for three months. Like all mothers, Jochebed thought her child was beautiful. She also must have had great faith, for she disobeyed the king's edict and resisted Pharaoh's power. When she could no longer hide her son, she laid him in a watertight basket and hid him among the reeds along the bank of the Nile. As a final precaution, she stationed her daughter, Miriam, nearby to watch.

At this point Jochebed had done all she could, and she trusted that God would miraculously provide the rest. And so it happened that Pharaoh's daughter and her entourage went down to the river to bathe and discovered the basket. When the princess opened the basket and saw the child crying, she felt sorry for him and recognized him as one of the Hebrew babies. Miriam was watching all this, no doubt with some fear. She came out and suggested, "Shall I go and get one of the Hebrew women to nurse the baby for you?" The princess told her to go, and Miriam went and called her mother. Pharaoh's daughter instructed Moses' mother to take the baby and nurse him, and even said she would pay Jochebed for her efforts.

This was incredible! After Moses' mother did everything possible, she gave God an opportunity to work, and God miraculously intervened. In fact, she was even rewarded financially for nursing her own child! When he was weaned, Moses was raised in the palace. Here the wealthiest, most powerful family in the land—and the enemies of God's chosen people—educated and trained the future deliverer of Israel. How can the birth, rescue, and upbringing of Moses be described in any way other than the work of God's providential care?

This story of the faith of Moses' mother gave me great courage and increased my faith. This woman did not abandon her child to fate. She did not cave in to Pharaoh's awesome power. She did not let the potential criticism of other women determine her course of action. She didn't calculate the odds in saving her own neck, and thereby take the quick and easy road. She didn't give up or give in to pressure, but gave *over* her child to God's custody. She did the *natural*, which allowed God to do the *supernatural*.

Moses' mother exchanged her own temporary security to do what she believed was right, and trusted the outcome to God. She performed her duty as best she could. I determined to follow her example. I would not give up my baby to fate. I would not surrender to the pressures of an intimidating bureaucracy. I would do everything possible to see that this child was raised in a Christian home, and then give it over to God's care. Perhaps my efforts wouldn't matter. Perhaps the keyboard operator wouldn't enter it into the computer. There was no way I could know that. But if I did all I could, I was willing to trust that God would have the child placed in the right home.

At my next meeting with "Colonel Caseworker," she stared me down and asked, "Now, are you going to give me any problems today?"

With my biggest smile I answered, "Not as long as that line about my child going into a Bible-believing home stays on the application."

She scowled at me, and I stared back. "Sign here," she snapped.

I signed the adoption papers with my notation on it, and sighed with relief. Mission accomplished.

As I waddled out of the agency that afternoon, I felt a peace that I had done all I could do. Maybe it wasn't much, but there was no limit to what my God could do.

He could intervene just as He had in the life of Jochebed and her son, Moses. Now all that remained was to deliver the baby.

Not long after I signed the final adoption papers I felt the first contractions of labor. Very early in the morning of February 11, 1964, I called for Mom Croft: "I think it's time to go to the hospital." Within ten minutes Mom and Dad were driving me to the country hospital. It was definitely not a General Hospital set. It was a large old gray building teeming with activity. I entered with a strange sense that I was delivering a precious package that didn't belong to me. This child belonged to the Lord. He had made plans for it.

I was in labor for 16 hours. Shortly before delivery I was given a general anesthetic, and when I woke up a couple of hours later, it was over.

I was wheeled up to a large ward where I waited to learn the results. Was it a boy or a girl? Was it healthy? Was it bald, like I had been for more than a year after my birth? Would I get to hold it? Or should I hold it? Maybe that would be too hard for me emotionally.

It wasn't long before I found out. An overweight nurse told me that I had given birth to a girl. "She's in good health," she reported matter-of-factly. "You'll be discharged tomorrow morning. Any questions?"

"Will I be able to see her?"

"No! That would cause problems. She'll be taken home in a couple of days. Now, you need to take these pills to dry up your breasts."

It didn't seem right that it should end so abruptly. But it was out of my hands now. I was free to go on with my life. As if nothing had ever happened? "She really is like Moses, Lord," I prayed. "She really is in Your hands. You can provide a 'Pharaoh's daughter' for my daughter." Much as my emotions were confused, I consciously reminded myself that this was *best* for the baby.

The next morning Mom Croft drove me home and I slept for most of the next two days. On the evening of the second night I sat at the kitchen table with Mom and Carol and talked about my future. "I'm going back to work in the morning," I announced.

"Are you sure you're ready?" Mom asked.

"Yes, the best thing for me to do now is get back to living a normal life. I'll certainly fit into the singles group a lot better now! But seriously, I've been thinking a lot about my future. Two of the girls in our singles group, Winnie and Rosalie, think I have leadership potential and that I should get more schooling. They've offered to help provide the funds for the first year of Bible school."

"Are you going to do it?" asked Carol.

"I'm applying at the Bible Institute of Los Angeles (now Biola). I'll work until then. I thought I'd share an apartment with one of the girls in the singles group until school starts."

"You know you're always welcome here if you need a good meal," said Mom.

"I know. I'll see you in church and we'll keep in touch. I'll never forget the love you've shown me." I had to stop for a moment to choke back the emotion that suddenly welled up in me. "You know, I've learned a lot from you and my situation. I've found that the things of God are often very hard to do at the beginning, but they are very easy and peaceful in the end. While the wrong choices are so easy to make at the beginning, but they end up so complicated and full of difficulties and regrets later. I want to thank you for helping me make the right choices . . . God's choices."

As I resumed work, it wasn't easy to bury the memory of my baby. I had to console myself by saying, "You'll have other children, Lee. This won't be the last." As I prayed for my child, I found that my greatest ambition for her was that she would come to know Christ. With that prayer came a sense of relief in my soul. I felt that I had done my *best* and that I could leave the *rest* to the Lord, and in this knowledge I gained a measure of satisfaction.

In the following weeks when I saw a mother with a

baby in the park or grocery store, I couldn't help but wonder if that was my baby girl. As the yearning would rise in my heart, I would pray for my daughter and her parents, reminding myself that she really wasn't my baby but the Lord's. It was His idea to create her, not mine, and He would be taking care of her from now on. Someday, I thought, I'll have a child of my own—in the right situation. Maybe it would be a little girl, and I would be able to raise her in the way that I wasn't capable of right now.

I could never escape the fact that a part of me was missing. But ironically, I felt no compulsion to fill that hole in my life. In one sense it didn't need to be filled, for while the baby was growing in me, God was patching the hole with His comfort. I thought of some of the pieces He had already fitted in. The lesson of forgiveness in the tacky motel room was a major piece. Learning to give thanks in my circumstances was another. Then came the realization that nothing passed God's desk without His approval, and that even a seeming disaster could fit His plan. I had also learned to release my problems to the Lord and allow Him to work after I had done all I humanly could.

It was true that part of me wanted to see my daughter, to find out how she was growing and learn the details of how God had provided for her needs. But I realized now that even if I never saw her, God would fill the void in my life.

Confirmation of that truth came from a wooden tract rack in the back of my church. One Sunday before the evening service I noticed a simple pamphlet with the title "The Weaver." As I read it, I felt that it was a perfect description of my life:

> My life is but a weaving between
>   my Lord and me;
> I cannot choose the colors He worketh
>   steadily.

The Missing Piece

Ofttimes He weaveth sorrow, and I
   in foolish pride
forget He sees the upper, and I the
   underside.

Not till the loom is silent, and the
   shuttles cease to fly,
shall God unroll the canvas and explain
   the reason why.

The dark threads are as needful in
   the weaver's skillful hand
as the threads of gold and silver in the
   pattern He has planned.

—Anonymous

There was my comfort. It didn't make any sense humanly, but it helped to know that there was a master plan. A chapter in my life had ended, but God saw the whole picture and how this episode fit in it. My prayer was that someday He would allow me a glimpse of the picture He saw on the upper side.

8

The "Prince" Arrives

Hal Ezell was a flashy dresser; his vogue style was in stark contrast to my "old maid" image. My bargain-basement specials could never complement his sharp attire. As I welcomed him to the convention in the lobby of a hotel in a suburb of Miami, the light reflecting off his white patent leather shoes and belt was anything but appealing to me. Yet he was good-looking and charming, and I couldn't ignore the twinkle in his eye as we talked. He had arrived from Los Angeles to attend a Spring, 1973 Bible conference that I was helping to coordinate.

Only a few weeks earlier our office had learned that Hal's wife, Wanda, had died within 24 hours of being admitted to an emergency room, leaving two daughters, ages 10 and 13. The cause of death was lupus disease. "We've been praying for you," I said as I introduced myself.

Hal expressed appreciation for my concern and invited me to join him for a sandwich in the coffee shop. "A lot of people all over the country have prayed for us," he said as we were seated. "I don't think we could have made it without those prayers."

"Actually, I have to be honest and say that I haven't been able to get you off my mind," I said, feeling a blush warm my face as I realized what I was saying. Hal and

I had met briefly before his wife's death during another conference in Southern California. Hal was a longtime vice president of a national fast-food chain, and also active in Christian work. His expertise in management and troubleshooting made him an outstanding businessman. He had helped arrange that Bible conference and his wife was scheduled to play the organ, but had to cancel at the last minute because of illness.

Ever since news of his tragedy had arrived at the Florida office, I had prayed that God would meet his needs and those of his two girls. But slowly my concern had grown into fascination. Despite my mental objections, I could not suppress the thought that God might have something in mind for us. Still, I hadn't planned to tell him so much.

Hal was not offended by my being so up-front. In fact he invited me to have dinner with him that night after the opening session. The rest of the day I battled conflicting emotions. I was 28 years old and involved in the ministry. After ten years on my own, I hadn't given up the hope that my prince might someday appear, but I was happily reconciled to living a single life.

For years I had constantly battled against a cynical attitude toward marriage. After all, I felt I was already a loser for being cheated out of my virginity and the opportunity to bear my first child for my husband. I figured that if I was honest with the man who would marry me, surely my past would disqualify me as a wife.

After moving to Florida in 1969 to work with a group that organized Bible conferences, I had stopped looking for a man, reasoning that no man was really looking for me. During the intervening years I had observed that making a marriage work was not that easy anyway, even for the most dedicated. I had ushered many unhappily married individuals into the counseling room. Often their problems seemed overwhelming, and the odds of their marriages surviving were against them.

Now I had met my potential prince-to-be, and he was not at all what I had envisioned, even in my wildest imagination. He was eight years older than I. He wasn't riding alone, silhouetted against the sunset, but had children in the saddle with him. Yet in spite of my efforts to suppress them, my romantic wonderings about Hal continued. True, he didn't fit my "Prince Charming" image, but I was discovering that he was a charming fellow and a prince of a guy. His dry wit was such a contrast to my slapstick humor, yet we seemed to complement each other.

Our dinner date was in a dimly lit restaurant, with candles giving a romantic atmosphere to each table. We enjoyed the evening so much that we agreed to spend some more time together. In fact, we ended up skipping much of the conference and spending most of the week enjoying the sights of Miami and sampling its finer restaurants.

However, sometimes our conversation had more of the feel of a job interview than a romantic discussion. The second evening he asked about my childhood, and I told him about growing up in the inner city, my father's drinking problem, my conversion at the Billy Graham Crusade, and the move west to San Francisco.

"Did you ever see your father again after you left Philadelphia?" Hal asked.

"No, I heard that he lived on the streets. I did write him once to tell him about how Christ changed my life and to say that I forgave him. But he never responded. Then one day, while I was in college, my Mom called to tell me she had just returned from my father's funeral. It turned out he had lived with Mom for the last few months when he was very sick from cirrhosis of the liver. But she never let me know until after he died."

"Where did you go to college?"

"Biola. I worked for a while before I went to school, so I was a couple of years older than everyone else in my class. I stayed just one year, then went to work as a secretary in a large church. I think that was the best thing that happened to me, for it gave me an opportunity to gain experience in the ministry. Instead of just pounding a typewriter all day, I also spent time counseling people who came in with problems."

As we ate, I mentioned that I remembered meeting him a few months earlier at the conference in California. "You were eating breakfast with your two daughters."

"That was a very difficult time. My wife was quite ill. By the way, you should know that Wanda Shows was my girls' second mother. Their real mother was a beautiful woman named Helen Gaffney. She died of a brain tumor when the children were three and six years old. Then I married Wanda and she helped me raise the children until she died very suddenly of lupus a few months ago. I admit my head is still spinning."

"How bizarre," I thought. "The next gal who marries this dude better get a complete physical!" I changed the subject by asking, "Do you have pictures of your daughters?" Hal pulled out his wallet and showed me a recent photo of lovely 13-year-old Pam. She had a winning smile, long brown hair, and a look of confidence. The picture of Sandi, age ten, showed her with a silly grin playing "adult" as she wore a wide-brim hat, a dress hanging almost to the floor, and high heels. "Where do they stay when you're away from home?" I asked.

"With my parents. For years my mother and father have pastored a church in the Los Angeles Harbor area." Hal was up-front in saying that he wanted to marry again, hopefully for the last time. "It's obvious that you're a sharp gal. I'm surprised some man hasn't grabbed you yet."

"I'm not enamored with marriage!" I stated emphatically.

But Hal didn't seem to hear me as he expressed the qualities he desired in a wife. "My next wife will have to fit into my world," he said. "She must be willing to move into our old house and fit the routine we have established. She has to love our girls." Almost as an afterthought he added, "I will have to love her, too."

His recitation turned me off, especially since I had not actually turned in an application. But since he mentioned some qualifications, I thought I'd mention a few of my own. "If I ever marry, I want to marry someone in Christian work where I can use my abilities in speaking, counseling, and music. I'm not one to sit on the sidelines."

"Good. I agree," he affirmed. "I think you should develop and use your God-given talents, as long as they don't detract from your first priority of husband and family."

This guy wasn't getting the message. Then I thought of something that I assumed would not fit into Hal's profile of the perfect wife. The next day I tested the waters by saying, "I need to be up-front with you. There's one phase of my life that I didn't mention." I swallowed hard and continued. "I had a baby out of wedlock about ten years ago. It was an ugly situation because I was raped by a man from work. I gave the baby up for adoption and never saw her, but I know she is out there somewhere. She was the vehicle God used to bring me to the end of myself and the beginning of my walk with Christ."

Hal appeared remarkably unshaken by the news. "I think it's great we can be so open with each other. I don't intend for this to end after I return to Los Angeles. I'm not your charismatic, charlatan playboy. I'm the marrying type."

I couldn't believe I remained a qualified "applicant," much less that I was actually falling for him. Indeed, the fascination quickly turned into romance. He was the finest caliber of man I had ever known. He was recognized in the ministry and business as a tough administrator, yet a man of integrity and sensitivity. And I experienced that sensitivity in our many long conversations.

That's not to say we didn't have some shaky moments. He also liked to tease me. He noted how my car, though new, was stripped bare, with no luxuries or accessories. It was all I could afford, and I didn't like being teased for living within my means.

However, most of the time we got along wonderfully, even though we were so different. Hal was from a totally different world than mine. Both of his parents were Assembly of God ministers. I couldn't believe that he had never even watched American Bandstand. That had been my whole world as a teenager. He was totally unimpressed that I enjoyed dancing, or that I was a pretty good cardplayer. He didn't know spades from shovels, clubs from diamonds. I teased him, "You were probably raised at a communion table between church services, while I was raised at a poker table between deals!"

When Hal returned to California, I still fought the fact that there was something wonderful happening. My friends said that this was God's doing. "No thanks," I responded. "I am not interested in being number three in a long line of dead wives. We're too different from each other, and I can't picture myself as 'mother.' I'm not the domestic type. The best thing I make for dinner is reservations."

Besides, it didn't seem proper. I thought of our parting conversation at the airport. Hal knew love was blossoming and told me, "I think there's something here. But it's going to be a long time before I can share this with my girls. They'll need time to prepare for another mother. That can't be done in an afternoon."

There were tears in this big guy's eyes as he said this, and I found myself choking back the emotion also. "I agree a hundred percent." I didn't even want to be mentioned to these beautiful girls because I was sure they would wonder what kind of hussy had latched on to their dear dad.

For the next few days our Florida-California phone bills were out of sight. As we talked, I realized I was committed to loving this fine man. Then just a week after he had left Florida, Hal phoned and said, "I've told the girls about you." Before I could respond, he put them on the phone to talk with me. My heart sank. "They'll hate me," I thought. Surely they were wondering who in the world Lee Kinney is, and why was she taking advantage of their grieving father.

"Hello, are you Lee?" said a sweet voice on the other line. It was Pamela Meliss Ezell. She began talking like a sophisticated young lady about her school and activities. Then Sandra Michele came on the phone. "My name is Sandi," said the warm, friendly voice. "Are you going to come and visit us?"

How was I to respond? I wondered how these girls could be so open to me when it was only a few months since they had put their second mother in the grave. I felt I was going off into the Twilight Zone, all my denial mechanisms in full operation. But I had to return to reality immediately when Hal came back on the phone. "Lee, I'd like you to move back to California."

I was stunned. "But . . . I can't just up and leave my job. And where will I live? I have to work. . . ."

"You can find work here in Los Angeles, and you can live with my parents. They have a nice home and you'll be very comfortable. I want the girls to get to know you. So come on out, piano and all."

The next week, the office where I worked gave me a going-away party. I sold my car, arranged for my piano and a few other belongings to be shipped, and flew back to California, my mind swirling with memories and questions. In one sense this was a sign of progress, since my trip west was now by plane rather than bus. But what would life hold for me? The first trip had ended in disaster.

Then it hit me. How ironic that I should have given away one daughter, and now I might be gaining two! That surely would demonstrate how no one can outgive God. I also noted that my natural daughter was one year younger than Hal's youngest daughter.

Hal's parents, Herb and Edna, lovingly received me. Nana and Papa, as they were affectionately known to me, checked me over thoroughly to make sure I fit the bill for wife number three. In the following months preceding our marriage, as I lived with Hal's folks, I learned a lot about Hal and his family. Soon a sparkling engagement ring rested on my left hand. One evening Hal said to me, "You were very bold in sharing your secret with me. I too need to share something with you. We will be unable to have any children of our own. Pam and Sandi are the only children we will share together." As I realized that my first baby would also be my last, somehow that baby became more precious.

It took time to assimilate into the family. Each of us struggled to adjust, I was stepparenting, Hal and the girls with their lingering grief. We all needed time for the inner healing of emotions that we knew only God could give us. Although they had many apprehensions, both girls were courageous in loving and accepting me during such a difficult period of their lives. There were many little things to work through, for this was a family that had already formed its habits, likes, and dislikes, and I hadn't figured in the picture. Their routine was established; I had to fit in. There was discussion about whether or not the girls would call me "Mom." They finally chose to do so and felt very comfortable with it. I was tickled that they wanted to do that, and it soon felt very natural.

I made every effort to make the transition as smooth as possible. Using some of my musical and dramatic abilities, I wrote a children's musical for their church and also composed "homemade" songs and skits for family birthday parties, Christmas parties, and other celebrations.

Our wedding day was beautiful and we all enjoyed it immensely. Hal and I walked down the aisle with our daughters, Pam and Sandi, as our only attendants.

On our wedding night I was overly apprehensive, as I imagine most brides must be. What would it be like to have sex with the man I loved? What could I expect from this man who was so experienced and knew how a wife was supposed to make love to him? I felt inadequate and inexperienced, and I figured I would just follow his lead. That was one of my best decisions.

I did not have any flashbacks of my rape experience during our first night because there was such tender loving care on Hal's part. He understood that it could have been a traumatic, repulsive thing and was sensitive to bring me along slowly.

It didn't take long to realize that I had worked harder at preparing for my wedding than our marriage! On the first morning of our honeymoon, when I figured I ought to wake up in the center of Hal's world, my husband's long arm reached across me to grasp the phone and talk to the girls before they left for school. Quickly my Prince Charming picture began to shatter. I had figured that I would be like Maria Von Trapp, marrying the Captain and dancing merrily over the hills with his children, as they did in "The Sound of Music." None of us could have counted the cost for the adjustments that would be necessary to fit us together into a well-oiled family.

I began to experience a monthly problem with U.M.S.—Ugly Mood Swings. In the weeks that followed, the girls realized that my role had changed. I was no longer "friend." I was "Mom"—that is, I was giving it my best shot. During my engagement I was simply a friend who came by to give advice, have fun, or go to a movie. Now suddenly this "friend" was issuing commands like "Get off the phone!" and "Go back upstairs and make your bed." There were some heated arguments. Like many a stepparent, I endured outbursts like "You're not my mother; I don't have to obey you!" That hurt, yet it was easy to forgive these girls because I knew that their anger stemmed from their grief and disappointment.

But there were plenty of fun times too as I saw these girls grow and mature. They were so different from each other. Spunky Sandi fluctuated between wanting to be a glamorous movie star or a crack softball player. Fun-loving and creative, she would compose "pretend songs" at the keyboard and sing them with gusto. Though she was compassionate and affectionate, she prevented dull moments with her quick wit.

Pam was a born leader. Even as a young teenager, her profound philosophical insights amazed us. She excelled in high school, and particularly loved her English classes. She had the ability to express her deepest thoughts and feelings through the melodies she composed on her guitar, alone in her room.

Had we known all the problems ahead of time, we might have chickened out. Yet those very experiences were the vehicles that God would use to bring us great blessing. I noted that this was a continuation of God's pattern as demonstrated in Scripture and in my own personal experience. "Divine irony," I called it.

9

Ghosts of the Past

Hal, his two daughters, and I stood as the judge entered the courtroom and made her way to her chair. With a nod of the head she acknowledged us and allowed us to be seated. Our legal counsel assured us that this was strictly a routine procedure, but my heart fluttered as I realized the authority this judge had. She was the one who would determine whether I could legally adopt Pam and Sandi as my own daughters.

I couldn't help but think of another couple many years ago who had gone through a similar process in adopting my baby. And I smiled as I realized again how they had been chosen by God, whether or not they even knew it, much as Pharaoh's daughter was chosen to fish Moses out of the Nile River. Now I was in an unusual position of adopting two girls after having put one girl out for adoption. Once I had trusted God to provide for my natural child that I was unable to provide for, and now God was trusting me to provide what these two beautiful girls needed—a loving mother.

During the first year of stepparenting we had our times of hand-to-hand combat. But now peace was settling into our relationship. Sandi sat on my left and reached for my hand while Pam on my right winked and whispered, "Aren't you glad you're not the wicked stepmother!"

The judge coolly asked me several routine questions: "How long have you known these girls? How do they address you?" The girls had to answer questions like, "Do you feel comfortable with Lee? What is your living situation like? Could you accept Lee as your adopted mother?" When it was over and the judge had officially decreed that I was now their mother, each of my daughters gave me a warm hug and whispered those precious words, "I love you, Mom."

There were many times when my mind flashed back to thoughts of my natural daughter. My early struggles as a stepparent made me wonder if my natural daughter knew she was adopted; if she knew, was she acting toward her stepparents as my girls were now? As my two adopted daughters matured and completed high school and then college, I was thrilled to see them become emotionally sound, and I prayed that the God who makes all things new would likewise erase any crippling effects from my natural daughter's past.

Now that I was married and part of a family that socialized with many other families, I found myself engaged in new activities that rekindled painful memories. Attending baby showers was particularly difficult. Besides all the dumb games with clothespins, diapers, and bottles, there was always the girl-talk:

"When are you due?" "Oh, you'll be late; the first one is always late." "Were you late, Lee?"

"No, I adopted my girls," I would answer.

"You mean you've never suffered through childbirth?" "Well, at least you got them without stretchmarks. . . ."

I would sit with a socially acceptable smile and listen to all the chitchat about labor pains and false trips to the hospital, feeling left out as the ladies discussed things I had supposedly never experienced. It was true that I had never become adept with diapers, bottle-warmers, or carseats, but I understood the emotions of giving birth and being a mother.

The emotions about my baby were also triggered

when I read magazine articles about adoptees or saw a news story or interview on television about a happy reunion between a child and her natural parents. I did not avoid these painful memories, but silently welcomed them and thanked God again for the guidance He had provided. Occasionally I would review my decision-making process, and I would always reach the same conclusion: I had done the right thing in 1964. There was a calm sense that because I had left my problem in God's "in" basket on His executive desk, I knew He had properly taken care of it. I was sure that it was properly logged into His omniscient computer memory system, where it would never be lost or forgotten. I had to believe that my faith had become the reality I had hoped for in my baby, even though I would probably never see the evidence with my human eyes.

One day I read in Ann Landers' column a birthday poem written by an adoptive parent who remembered the price the natural mother paid so her child could have a better life. When I would silently remember my daughter's birthday, I would reread this heartfelt poem and pray for my girl and her parents:

A BIRTHDAY

It's my child's birthday.
I have no memories of his life growing inside
    me and fighting to be released.
Another someone was there.
Another someone somewhere is feeling
    emptiness inside.
I'm sure she is wondering
Who he looks like.
If he is big or small.
Wondering if he laughs much.
It's my child's birthday.
And in the midst of this blessed day that was
    given to me
I have a prayer.

Oh, God, that I may never forget that someone
   suffered so much to give life to my child.
That someone loved my child so very much that
   she gave him the right to live.
May I never forget for a moment and especially
   now, today, to offer a prayer of thanks for
   that someone, and that You, dear God, will
   always be there for that someone to help her
   through the hurts she will have when she
   stops to think that today is "my child's
   birthday." Amen.

—Ann Landers
© News America
Syndicate

It was true that I thought of my baby on her birthday
and many other occasions, but there was no stabbing
sense of pain in the remembrance. It was as if I had a
scar on my hand that reminded me of an old, deep cut.
The memory remained, but the pain was gone. I realized
that this was a missing piece in my life. There were many
unanswered questions. Yet I felt whole, for God had
taught me things that I had used as mortar to plug this
hole in my life. I now realized that this and other problems in my life were "custom-made" situations designed
to take me into a deeper relationship with God. Rather
than resisting them, I could look for the purpose in them.

An old saying often helped me remember this truth:
"God fixes a fix to fix you. If you fix the fix before you
are fixed, He will have to fix *another* fix to fix you."

It took a fresh "fix" to show me just how much God
had already done in my life. One day while playing racquetball I was accidently hit in the head by the ball. For
1½ years I experienced a pain in the upper right side of
my face. I visited a number of specialists trying to determine whether it was caused by my teeth, jaw hinge,
sinuses, ears, or something else. Finally I was referred

to the pain center at the University of California Medical Center.

I was so naive at the time that I didn't realize that the first person who sees you is a psychiatrist. Doctor Levy seemed overly friendly, and I assumed she was chatting with me to fill in time before I began the physical examinations. She asked me questions about my past, and after nearly an hour I began to get the picture. Her job was to put pressure on me to discover something in my past which could cause my present pain.

As she summed up my story, she said, "So you are the middle child then, correct?"

"If number three of five is the proverbial middle child, then I'm it," I replied testily. While I had answered her questions about my past, I actually didn't tell her even half of the facts.

Doctor Levy continued, "Then you were a rejected child, abused and raised in poverty with an abusive father. Can you ever remember your father hitting you very hard on the right side of your face?"

"No, not really."

"When you were hit in the racquetball accident, the person who hit the ball was a man. Did you think of your father at that time?"

"Certainly not! I was almost unconscious on the floor."

She continued pressuring me for more than an hour in an effort to trigger a memory or emotional response which would point to unresolved bitterness that could cause my present pain. After I reviewed my glossary of emotional traumas with her, she pressed for the kill: "Be honest with me, Lee. Don't you have a secret fear that there's a cancerous tumor on the right side of your face and you will also die, being the third wife to fail your husband and children?"

I'm not sure I can call it righteous indignation, but I rose up in my seat and decided to give her the straight scoop. "Listen, Dr. Levy, I know what you're getting at. I've learned what bitterness and anger and unforgiveness can do to a person. I've gone through a process of cleansing and forgiveness that has made a difference. Because of my relationship with Jesus, the Messiah, I honestly have no lingering effects from the injustices of my past!"

Dr. Levy scribbled some notes in her file, probably something like, "She's a Jesus freak, too . . ." After two more visits, she apparently became convinced that my pain was not psychologically induced. She even issued a written report confirming that my elevator did go all the way to the top. Members of the surgical staff then did exploratory surgery and found the physical cause of the pain. A chronic infection had been festering, compounded by teeth puncturing the sinus cavity and chronic infection from two inflamed root canals. Surgery corrected these problems, and I haven't suffered from that pain since. But if I had not been an emotionally healed person through the power of the Lord, I might still be sitting in that psychiatrist's office and then paying her exorbitant bills while still hurting on the right side of my face!

It was many experiences like this that motivated me to begin sharing the lessons of my life with other people. I knew of many women who were looking to their analysts for answers. They were discovering past experiences that could explain the pain they felt. But understanding their past didn't remove the pain. Many of them could not cope with their guilt and deep-seated bitterness and frustration. Maybe some of the answers I had discovered in coping with my pain could help.

As I had opportunities to speak to various women's groups and Bible studies, a message began to crystallize. In it I would share my weakness and assure my audience that I did not have it all together. "At least, if I did, I forgot where I put it."

Through my personal experience, I related how for many years I had suffered from fantasy thinking. On the bus trip west I had envisioned living a life free of pain in the land of promise. That dream was cruelly dashed.

The Missing Piece

I had imagined I would marry and wake up each morning with fresh breath, to be served eggs Benedict by my prince. Instead, reality for me was moving into a bedroom where another wife had lain on the mattress, surrounded by gaudy flocked wallpaper of yet another wife's choosing.

I recalled the day we had ordered a new mattress. As the furniture movers picked up the old mattress and carried it out the door, I noted that a greeting card envelope had been hidden on top of the box springs. I eagerly opened the envelope, tickled because Hal seldom did unexpected things like this for me. Inside was a romantic card about love, and how "we two were meant for each other." It was signed "Love, Wanda."

Everywhere ghosts of the past were lurking. I could not alter the past, but I could seek for strength and wisdom to deal with the past, present, and future. Early in my marriage I relied on the verse "This is the day which the Lord has made; let us rejoice and be glad in it."[1]

This was different from fairy-tale thinking that latched on to the line "and they lived happily ever after." I was breaking free of my Cinderella thinking and learning to be content in whatever state I found myself. Yes, there were missing pieces in my life, but God had substituted His peace for those empty holes.

Every woman I met had some missing pieces in her life, and I seemed to have the kind of face people liked confessing to. After I had spoken to a women's group in Southern California, a woman came up to tell me about her missing pieces—unanswered questions from a divorce, a rebellious child, and most recently a car accident. "I just can't take it anymore," she cried. "What is God trying to do to me? Sometimes I think I'm being punished for my past sins." She stopped to wipe her tears and blow her nose. "You see . . . many years ago I had a baby . . . and I gave it up for adoption."

My heart sank when I heard those words. How could this woman possibly imagine that the "counselor" sitting in front of her also suffered through the same experience in life? "Please stop punishing yourself," I pleaded. "Jesus died and paid the price for your sins so you wouldn't have to pay for the rest of your life. God does want your attention, but you're not on parole with God. He is not breathing down your neck and catching you at every turn."

And then for the first of many times in individual counseling, I shared the story of the birth of my daughter. I noticed a gleam in her eye as she tearfully listened, and I realized for the first time that it was the very experiences of my past which now qualified me to speak to this woman's fears. The truth that I had learned could enable her to be free and have hope for the future.

I began writing down many of these helpful principles for improving relationships with God, ourselves, and other people, and wound up having them published in a book called *The Cinderella Syndrome*. In it I briefly revealed my rape experience, but since there was never any resolution to that experience, I stopped short of reporting my pregnancy and subsequent placing of my baby for adoption. Perhaps there was fear in sharing it. It might make me vulnerable to further hurt. And though God filled the void in my life with His peace, I knew that somewhere in this country was a young woman, my daughter, who was now approaching her twenty-first birthday. How could I tell this story without knowing what happened to her?

10

The Silence Is Broken

Hal was back East on one of his frequent trips. For the last couple of years he had served as a political appointee in the Reagan administration, with the title of Commissioner of Immigration for the Western Region of the United States. He had his hands full! But he considered it as God's challenge for his life. I was glad this would be his last trip of the year, though there were only three weeks left.

I had spent the day and much of the evening doing some Christmas shopping and had stopped on the way home to pick up food. As I came into the house and set down two bags of groceries, I noticed that the red light was blinking on the phone-answering machine. As I began to play back the messages I heard a familiar sound from the past. It was the sweet, shaky old voice of Mom Croft, now 80 years old. "Well, Honey, this is Mom Croft and I hate talking into these dumb machines. But I have a very important message for you, and I think you should call me right away."

"Something's happened to Dad Croft," I thought as I immediately dialed her number. "Hi, Mom, this is Lee," I said, trying not to sound too worried.

"Oh, Honey, I'm so glad you called, 'cuz I, Dad and me, have been a-prayin. We didn't know what to do.

We got this here letter and I didn't know whether I should call you or not . . ."

I interrupted to ask, "What are you talking about?"

"The letter! I got a letter from your daughter!"

My knees buckled and my mind felt like it was being enveloped by the fog rolling to start another "Twilight Zone" episode. My normally glib tongue was silent.

"We've had this letter for two weeks, and I been fixin' to call you," Mom continued. "I didn't know if your husband knew about your past and I didn't want to cause any problems. But Dad and me been a-prayin', and we decided we should call and let you know and you can decide what to do about it."

"I . . . I don't know what to say. It's been 20 years. She just wrote to you out of the blue?"

"I got a phone call several weeks ago from a young woman who asked, 'Do you know anyone by the name of Lee Kinney?' " Of course I wanted to know what she wanted before I gave her any information, and she says, 'I'm searching for her. She's my birthmother.' I was so shocked I said, 'No, I've never heard of her,' and hung up. Well, next week she calls again, and before I can say anything she says, 'Excuse me, my name is Julie. I'm calling again because I think you do know how to locate my birthmother, Lee Kinney.' I told her, 'Look, I'm not getting involved. I can't say anything one way or another.' "

"Her name is Julie," I said absentmindedly.

"She was real persistent. She pleaded with me. 'If I simply send you a letter, could you get it to her? I've been searching for her, and I believe you know how to reach her. But I'll leave it in your hands.' She said I could forward the letter to you, but if I didn't, she wouldn't bother me again. I didn't know what to say, so I said, 'I can't promise you anything, Honey.' She said that was okay, she just wanted to send the letter in case I knew where to locate you, and so she sent this letter and I thought I ought to let you know."

"Hold on, Mom, I need to sit down." I pulled up a chair and collapsed in it.

"I hope I did the right thing," Mom said.

"Yes, you did the right thing. What does the letter say?"

"Do you want me to read it to you?"

"Please. If you don't mind."

And so Mom started reading the letter, dated November 23, 1984.

Dear Mr. and Mrs. Croft,

I am writing to you in response to the phone call we had last week. I hope you will take the time to read this letter and think it over carefully.

For more than three years I have been looking for my natural parents. And a couple of weeks ago I received some medical records that had your phone number on it, so I decided to call. I believe you know my mother, Miss Lee Kinney. I didn't expect to reach anyone at your number, and so I wasn't really prepared to discuss the situation very well. I hope this letter will fill in the blanks for you.

The first concerns of mine are that I don't cause anyone any trouble, and that I don't disrupt anyone's life. I am sure that if I don't handle the situation properly there could be a lot of hurt people, and that's the last thing I want to do. I really want to get in touch with my mother, but I think my feelings come last.

When I was 15 my adoptive parents decided to move from California to Michigan. In the summer of '81 I got married, and in May of this year we had our first child, and her name is Casey. So my mother is also a grandmother.

I was hoping you could maybe give me some information about my mother. I have a lot of questions that I hope you can answer. I realize that it has been a long time, but anything you could tell me would be appreciated.

I understand that my mother was very talented. Do you know if she made a career out of those talents? If you have any pictures of Lee I would like to have one if it's possible. I would appreciate anything you could tell me about my mother, or anything you think I should know.

I have always known that I was adopted, and my adoptive parents are supportive of me in my search. Love is the only reason that I am searching. Unlike other adoptees, I have never had any harsh feelings about my natural parents. I know that if I hadn't been brought up in a Christian home my feelings toward my birthparents would be different.

I feel the Lord guiding me in my search, and that He will also help me make the right decisions. You will not hear from me again unless you contact me.

God Bless You.

Julie

This was beyond belief. The mere thought that my "baby" could be writing this letter was beyond comprehension. Why hadn't she grown up in my imagination? In my mind she was still a child, not a full-grown married woman with a child of her own. I couldn't imagine her as a person who could express herself so well on paper. And her baby made me a grandma!

Mom Croft's voice jolted me back to reality. "I'm sorry, Sweetie," she blurted. "I hope this don't cause a problem for you. Dad and me wasn't sure whether to tell you, but we thought you should decide whether to contact her." Then dear old Mom, as only she could do, couldn't resist giving me her opinion. "I sure would call her, Darlin', cause she says she believes the Lord is leading her to find you. Isn't that somethin' else?"

I couldn't help laughing at her enthusiasm. "Yes, Mom, it's something else. Something right out of this world!" She had Julie's address and phone number, and I carefully wrote them down and repeated them back. Then I agreed to let her know what happened, and we hung up. For a long time I stared into the fireplace as though it were a black hole in space, wishing it would swallow me up. A tingling sensation spread throughout my body, adding to my feeling of "otherworldliness."

Yes, this was something out of this world. Had my daughter, like I, had a divine intervention in her life? I knew in my heart that because of my pregnancy I began to walk in a daily, living relationship with Jesus Christ. Now I wondered why she had said, "I feel the Lord guiding me." What did this all mean?

I began to cry, tickled with joy and yet paralyzed with fear at the same time. Conflicting emotions began to run through me. "This is terrific . . . but on the other hand, it could produce some real problems . . . but on the other hand, what a blessing. . . ." I was elated to the point of laughing, yet at the same time I was cautious. What would be the outcome of all this? Was this a dream, or a nightmare?

"Why do things go crazy when my husband is away?" I thought. This was one night when I didn't want to be alone. But I had no choice. He wouldn't return until tomorrow afternoon.

So I had to turn to God, as I had so many times before. In my mind I visualized the scene of a request being placed on God the Father's executive desk 3½ years earlier. It read, "I want to find my birthmother" and was signed "Julie." I imagined this and many subsequent requests receiving the same big rubber stamp "No." The time was not right. Then one day, just a few weeks ago, God received that request again, and this time He stamped it with a big green "Yes" and the missing pieces began to fall into place.

So I needed to accept the idea that my daughter's getting in touch with me was all in the Lord's timing and for a purpose. Still, I was worried. There were all kinds of concerns about the effect that this interruption would have on my life and the life of my family. But our heavenly Father knew what was best for me, for Julie, and for everyone else concerned. He wouldn't permit us to face anything we couldn't handle. So He allowed Julie to contact me.

"I've got to tell Hal," I thought. "This can't wait until tomorrow." I dialed my husband's hotel number back East, hoping he was in his room. It turned out I had roused him from sleep. "Wake up enough for me to tell you something important," I said. "Listen! I've received a letter from that baby I had out of wedlock over 20 years ago," I blurted out.

"Say that again!" I could tell I had Hal's full attention. After I briefly told him about the phone call from Mom Croft, his first reaction was similar to mine. "I don't believe it."

"It's true. She's living in Michigan. I have her name, phone number, and address. I'm scared. I'm thrilled. And I wish you were here." Then I added proudly, "And I'm a grandmother! What do you say to that, Grandpa?"

"Wait a minute!" he shot back, not wanting to agree with that idea too quickly. "Let's think this thing through." Then he sensitively added, "What would you like to do?"

"I want to contact her, of course! But I can't imagine what that will lead to. What do you think?" I hoped he would take the lead and share some of the responsibility.

Hal did take the lead, but his answer showed me who led him. "The Lord said 'Yes,' so I think you should say 'yes' and call her in the morning. Whatever you decide to do, I'll back you a hundred percent," he assured me.

After we concluded our conversation, I got up to walk out of the den and looked at the parchment plaque hanging on the wall. The message was never more pertinent than now:

If you love something
Set it free.
If it comes back,
It is yours.
If it doesn't,
It never was.

I had loved one baby and set her "free." Now this baby was a grown woman, coming back to me with another baby in her arms. And tomorrow I would talk to her.

11

Questions, Questions

That night there was very little sleep and no rest for me. Mom Croft's phone call had put my mind on fast forward. Thoughts were racing through without stopping for consideration or answers. "What is she like?" "What is her *real* motive for searching for me?" "Was this the Lord's way of making real to me the principle of sowing and reaping, and now I would see what I had sown by giving away the baby?" "Why did she marry at 17?" "Was she unhappily married?" "Was her marriage an escape?" "Had she felt rejection, loss, and depression because she was not wanted at birth?" "Was this her way of starting a new life out West—in Tinseltown?"

It was my natural tendency to let my imagination project possible future scenarios. When my husband was late in getting home from work, I would begin wondering if he was involved in an accident on the freeway. When the phone rang, I was sure it was the paramedics. As it got later, I pictured myself racing to some remote hospital. I even saw myself dressed in black at the funeral . . . and I looked elegant.

That night on my bed, my wild imagination projected all kinds of possible events. Maybe Julie was depressed because of an unbearable life, and thought that a meeting with her "real" mother would give her life new meaning. What if she wanted to come out here and live with me? Perhaps this now-grown baby wanted to turn her own baby over to me to raise. At 40 years of age, how would I do with a baby? And then, how would my two daughters react to this shock?

What would I say when Julie asked about her natural father? How could I tell her she was the result of an assault, an accident that should never have happened? Wouldn't that just add to her feelings of rejection and remorse? "No!" I told myself, "I must never tell her that she was conceived in rape."

Then I thought about Julie's adoptive parents. They were not Julie's natural parents, just as I was not the natural mother of Hal's daughters. But I considered myself the mother of Hal's girls, having lived with them and invested myself in them over the years. Likewise I had to consider Julie's parents, who had raised her from birth, to be her real mother and father.

So where did I fit in? Wouldn't I be a great interruption in her life and a threat to her parents, who had given themselves to her for more than 20 years? Though I wasn't the natural mother of my two girls, I would fight tooth and nail against any woman who knocked at my front door to announce that she was their "real mother." How could this possibly be resolved?

I thought about my right to privacy. Could someone unknown to me dig into the deep dark secrets of my past without my permission? Weren't there laws that protected me from this? But then I thought, "Yes, you have rights as a birthparent, Lee. But they are not exclusive of the rights of the child. That baby did not participate in any confidentiality agreement. No one had the right to promise that she would not begin a search later in life." The laws of confidentiality were set up to protect this transaction from curious outsiders, not from the immediate parties involved.

By morning, when it was time to get out of bed, my energy allotment for the day was already spent. With great effort I forced myself up to a sitting position on the edge of the bed. For several minutes I stared at the phone number scratched in black on the yellow tablet on my nightstand. What did that number really represent? If I called, what kind of an interruption would that bring into my life? Or was this a wonderful divine interference?

I realized that I had not made the mistake of suspending my life, waiting for this moment. Though I had lived 20 years with this missing piece, I felt whole. It wasn't simply a system of denial, where I submerged the hurts of the past. I had truly resolved my problem, and the missing piece of my past had been filled with the peace of God. So what did it mean now that He was revealing that missing piece?

The weight of all these questions motivated me to speak aloud with Jesus. "Well, Lord, You know all the questions racing through my mind. And You already know all the answers. I really want to meet Julie, but where will this lead? I can't count the cost, and neither can Hal. What will it mean to Pam and Sandi? I don't know the answers, but I believe You have said, 'Yes, now is the time.' So I will agree with You and make the call."

Still, I could not stop brooding over these questions as my finger started dialing the telephone number in Michigan. As the phone started ringing, my pounding heart increased its tempo.

A sweet voice on the other end answered, "Hello."

I swallowed hard and said, "Is this Julie?"

She answered with a restrained, "Yes."

"Well, I hope you're sitting down because this is Lee calling."

There was a gasp in her voice as she said, "Oh, I knew you would call someday! I'm just glad *you* called *me* because I wouldn't know what to say."

"Now you know how I feel!" I admitted, a bit relieved.

In the background I heard a baby cry. Could that

be my grandchild? Julie excused herself to quiet the baby. When she returned, she asked brightly, "Well, what do we do now?"

"I don't know." I hesitated, "How in the world did you find me?"

She reached for a folder that was near the phone and began to describe the papers she had gathered as a result of her search. "My mother gave me the adoptive papers a week after I was married. During my 3½-year search, I wrote a lot of letters, and finally received help from ALMA. Have you ever heard of them?"

"No, I haven't."

"They're the Adoptive Liberty Movement Association in California. They help adoptees trace their birthparents. Then I called the hospital where I was born and the Los Angeles County adoption agency. Everything fell into place, though, when I spoke with Mrs. Croft."

"How did you find out about her?" I inquired.

"On one of the papers there was an old phone number where you could be reached. Since it was 20 years ago, I figured you were no longer there, but I thought there was a possibility that someone might know who you were and where I might find you. I guess Mrs. Croft gave you my message."

I was immediately relieved, then thrilled that Julie did not seem like an unhappy, distressed, melancholy person. Rather, her voice revealed a sensitive young woman with a delightful personality. It seemed from the mellow tone of her voice that this was not a desperate search. Rather, she was knocking on my door—appropriately and lightly—to see if I would open it.

Early in our conversation I sheepishly admitted to Julie that I had noted some of the dates in her letter and figured that she must have been married at the age of 17. I didn't express my secret fears that she might have "had to get married."

She sweetly replied, "We knew it was—I don't know if you can understand this or not—but we knew it was the will of God for us to marry." I stifled a gasp. Did I hear her right? She said it was *God's will.*

She continued, "We've been married three years and have a nine-month-old daughter. Do you hear her crying in the background? That's your granddaughter, Casey." It was a curious feeling to hear the voices of three generations all meeting for the first time on this telephone line.

Julie then began to read to me from the papers she had collected. She asked me about my mother and four sisters, supplying me with their current names and addresses and other information. It was shocking to realize that so much personal information was on computers. Julie admitted that the material she had received was far in excess of what she had asked for or was necessary.

Then the inevitable question came: "What can you tell me about my natural father?"

"What information do you have?" I reluctantly replied, determined to hold fast to my decision not to reveal my secret.

"One set of papers indicated that at the time I was conceived, my father was 38. Another set of papers says 48, which would have made him either 20 or 30 years older than you. Which was he?"

"I don't know." I replied, dreading what was ahead.

"Did you ever meet his mother and father, who lived in Kansas City?"

"No," I acknowledge, trying to appear casual.

"Did you ever meet any of his four other children?" she persisted.

I was hearing all of these facts for the first time. I swallowed hard and said, "No, I didn't."

"Did you know him when he was a truck driver or pilot? Did you know him when he was in the Navy or in the construction business?"

"No," I repeated. Fortunately, the personal questioning about her natural father subsided. I couldn't tell what she surmised from my lack of information. I quickly changed the subject to inquire about her baby.

A moment later she suddenly asked, "How do you feel about me searching for my natural father?"

"That's totally up to you. Whatever you want to do, you should go ahead and feel free to do it." This was beginning to hit too close to home. The questions about her father drained me of energy and emotion. I was surprised that the stress of 21 years ago could still affect me so much.

Fortunately Julie's conversation took a different tack, one which began to lay a common ground between us other than biological. She began to tell me of her love for music, something which no one else in her family shared. She told me about the three different singing groups she had joined through her church. Eagerly my mind took off in another flight of imagination and I had to warn myself, "Don't jump to conclusions. She could be in some cult."

"Julie, can you tell me what kind of church you're in?"

"I don't know if you'll understand this, but my pastor was ordained in the Foursquare denomination. We are what you would call a 'charismatic' church. Have you heard of that before?"

Her reply overwhelmed me. Hal and I had been active in charismatic churches for many years. His father was ordained in the Assemblies of God. My mind left our conversation for a moment as I thought back to my request on her adoption papers. I had asked that she be raised in a Bible-believing home. ("Thank You, Lord!") My deepest desire and prayer had been answered, in spite of all odds—including "Colonel Caseworker."

When my mind returned to Julie, I heard her saying, ". . . why I have kept up my search for you is because I had to know if you had surrendered your life to Christ."

Nothing could have hit me more forcefully. I was being witnessed to! The one who had led witnessing teams, who had attempted to be a witness for Christ on the street, in the office, and over radio and television. For once my motormouth was speechless. No other good news could have equaled what that question revealed about Julie.

I must have muttered something, for Julie went on to tell me that she had been raised in a Christian home. Her father, Harold, had two children before his first wife passed away. He then married Eileen and they decided to enlarge their family circle by adopting a baby girl.

As Julie continued relating the details of her life, I learned she had been raised about 40 miles from where I had lived and worked. As she began to identify the town and neighborhood, I recognized that it was the same area where my sister, Zoe, and her family had lived after they moved from San Francisco. It's possible that they might have seen each other many times. Perhaps, as I was driving through the neighborhood to my sister's house, I had seen Julie playing in a yard or street with friends.

There was an eagerness now for us to arrange a face-to-face meeting, yet both of us were hesitant to push for that right away. I was particularly concerned for Julie's parents. I owed them so much; how could I think of hurting them? Yet how could I deny the wishes of my own daughter? "What do your parents think about your search for me?" I asked.

"At first my mom didn't want me searching for someone who didn't want me. But now that I'm older, and I'm married and have a baby, she feels fine about it."

"Do you mind if I ask how you found out that you were adopted?"

"I was very young. I was playing with a little girlfriend and she told me that my mother was not my 'real mommy.' I went running home and asked my mom, 'Is it true you are not my real mommy?' That's when she explained that I was adopted.

"You know, I just recently realized something. Ever since I can remember, Mom bought my shoes at Kinney Shoe Stores. Maybe she thought it would help you in some way, since your maiden name was Kinney."

Hopscotching again to another subject, Julie threw

out this question: "What do you do with your time now that your two girls are raised?"

This was a question I was ready for. In anticipation, I was almost giggling as I responded, "I am an inspirational speaker who shares the goodness of God with groups across the nation in retreats and conferences. I have a national radio ministry, and I've just written a book called *The Cinderella Syndrome* which I hope God will use to bring people to faith in Christ."

Between gasps and giggles, Julie expressed, "Isn't God great the way He works!"

"Julie, a little earlier you wanted to lead me to Christ. I was speechless because . . . in a way, I can say that it *was* you who led me to Christ over 20 years ago."

As Julie listened 2000 miles away, I tearfully told her my story, concluding, "I gave you *natural birth*. But God used you to awaken my *spiritual life!*"

We had talked for an hour-and-a-half, and it was time for us to wind down the conversation. We pledged to keep in touch and consider the next step in this new-found relationship. Before saying our goodbyes, I asked, "Julie, will you please reassure your mother and father that I in no way intend to make a big intervention in their lives?"

"Yes, I will do that," she assured me.

My stomach was full of butterflies as we hung up. But at least they were learning to fly in formation! In less that 24 hours I had acquired a third grown daughter, a son-in-law, and a granddaughter. That's what I call fast work!

I felt satisfied. Complete. An original piece from the puzzle had been dropped into place. I couldn't wait to tell somebody. While I was on the phone, Dee, my secretary, had come into the office I have at home. "You were on the phone for quite a while," she said.

"Sit down! Have I got something to tell you!"

As I told her my story from the beginning, she began to cry. I couldn't believe the impact it had on her. When

I finished, she said, "That's incredible. I hope you're going to tell that when you speak."

"I'm not ready to do that yet," I said.

"But just think of the hope this can give to so many people! It shows how when someone trusts God and commits a problem to Him, He is faithful to work it all out," Dee enthusiastically replied.

"Yes, but I need time to sort all this out. It's happened so suddenly. Julie and I haven't even met yet."

As I continued to reflect on the incredible experience of talking to my natural daughter, I suddenly realized, "Pam! Sandi! What are they going to think about all this?" I had never discussed this part of my life with them. Now I would have to tell them the truth. How would they handle this news?

12

Tender Disclosures

How I wish I had told my daughters about my secret! But I had thought there was no reason to do so. What purpose would it serve? It was only an incomplete episode out of my life, one with no resolution. Doesn't everyone have some secret thing in her past? Doesn't every woman have a skeleton or two hidden in her closet? I had rationalized that my experience would only instill an unhealthy fear of dating and a mistrust of men. But now what if the girls would be hurt wishing that they had been given the chance to love me, beyond my skeletons?

Now I was beginning to realize that this decision was a mistake. I should have known better. Too often I had seen other people make the mistake of not dealing with a problem openly, pretending that everything was okay. A woman who was dating pretended she was not divorced. A businessman concealed a past bankruptcy from his partners. A wife hid her checking account overdrafts from her husband. A husband avoided communicating his feelings of inadequacy to his wife. Parents of an adopted child pretended they were the natural parents. In each case, discovery of the truth only complicated matters and intensified the hurt, whereas if it has been honestly confessed at the beginning, it might well have strengthened the relationship.

It was too late for me to think now of what I should have done. I needed to share my secret with my daughters. Hal called Pam at her office and asked her to come by the house after work. "Is it something bad?" she asked. "It must be some bad news."

"I can't tell you right now. But come as soon as you're off work. We're going to ask Sandi to do the same."

When Hal called Sandi, she asked, "Did you get a promotion? Are you moving to Washington D.C.?"

"No, no," he replied. "We're not moving. But we need to talk with you and Pam, so please come by tonight."

Hal arrived home midafternoon and I filled him in about my phone conversation with Julie. He was concerned about the meeting with the girls. "You need to realize that they're expecting something bad. Remember, twice they've been called to a family meeting like this, and it began, 'Your mother has been very sick . . .' They're no doubt apprehensive. They've already lost two mothers, so they may not be too thrilled when they learn they're not your only daughters."

It hurt to realize how insensitive I'd been. I had known about this for 20-plus years, and Hal for 11. We had had time to adjust. But Pam and Sandi didn't have that advantage. How could they possibly anticipate the shock of having someone enter their lives, someone they had never realized was standing in the shadows all these years?

That evening the four of us sat in the den. Fear and worry clawed at me as I began to recite the story of what had happened to me when I was 18 years old. Pam and Sandi kept their eyes riveted on me as they fought back tears. When I completed the story with the phone call I had made that morning, there was total silence. The bomb had been dropped.

Finally I couldn't stand it any longer. "What do you think?" I asked. "Talk to me. What do you have to say?"

Sandi, the younger, spoke first. "I think it's great, Mom! It's just like the soap operas. I know you don't like them, but that's the way life is. A new character is written into the story as the baby of the leading lady. It's a great story!"

"Well, that lightens my load," I thought. "At least she sees something amusing in it." But then, maybe her humor was just a way of reducing the tension. She was always able to see the lighter side of things.

Meanwhile Pam sat silently, projecting what all of this meant for the future of the family. Unlike her mom, Pam always had her mind in gear before her tongue was engaged. "Well, I don't think it's so great," she finally said tearfully. "Why didn't you tell us about this before?"

I felt my palms sweating and my stomach churning. It felt exceptionally warm in the room. Pam tearfully continued, "You should have told us before. What do you expect us to say? That we're overjoyed?" My fears were being realized. I was crushed that they couldn't share in my joy. I tried to listen as the emotions of our meeting began to crescendo in a barrage of questions.

"She's not going to come here, is she? She's going to stay in Michigan, right?"

"We didn't talk about that," I answered nervously. "She has a family, so I assume they'll remain in Michigan."

"Do we have to meet her? Will she call you 'Mom'?"

"You don't have to meet her." At that point the discussion dwindled to a halt.

Hal diplomatically closed our time together by saying, "Your mother and I don't expect you to jump for joy at this news. I think we should give you girls time to think this through and then we should discuss it another time."

As my daughters left the house that night, I hugged them and said again that I loved them. I could tell by their eyes and their hesitant hugs that this was more difficult for them to handle than either Hal or I had anticipated. My girls had already lost two mothers. Were they afraid of losing a third mom to a "real daughter"?

Even though they were grown and independent, they were afraid that some natural daughter would prance onto the stage like a little lost princess, holding the first grandchild, and overtake their places in my heart. It was all too sudden and unreal to them. Their reactions were reasonable, and I knew that behind their feelings were hearts of love for me. We had been knit together as one family regardless of who was the natural mother to whom.

That night I went to bed with a load of apprehension. "Lord, I know You brought this about, and I know You will work things out," I prayed. "For 20 years when I didn't worry, You cared for everything. Why do I think my worrying will help now? I've got to trust You to work this out too."

One thing that was hard to accept was the fact that I was a grandmother. I expressed that to Hal and he said in his typical direct style, "Well, that doesn't make me a grandfather. That girl wasn't my baby. I didn't have anything to do with it, so I am not a grandfather." I wondered if this was an expression of resentment or just a refusal to admit that we were both getting older. Or maybe it was just that he had long awaited the day when one of his own daughters would present him with a grandchild.

But Hal was supportive of my continued communications with Julie. Telephone calls, along with letters between Michigan and California, began to fill in the 20-year gap. Every new piece of information disclosed how faithful God had been in watching over this baby I had committed to His care.

In one conversation I hesitantly asked Julie whether or not she suffered from many of the physical weaknesses that were apparent in my family. "Do you have any sinus problems?" I asked. "No," she replied.

"Any intestinal problems, like with digestion?"

"No, I don't think so."

"How about arthritis?"

"Not that I'm aware of. I'm pretty young yet, and I'm quite healthy."

I was grateful that she seemed not to have gained any of my physical weaknesses. And secretly I thought that maybe, since I didn't raise her, she might have also avoided some of my nonphysical weaknesses, such as a stubborn streak and a tendency to talk too much.

There was one major disagreement between Hal and me. Hal insisted that I needed to tell Julie that she was the product of a rape. I disagreed. "How could you tell someone that she was conceived under circumstances like I experienced?" I argued.

"Because you need to make it clear that you are not the type of girl who was just sleeping around and got caught," he answered.

"Don't you understand what that would mean to Julie? It could be devastating."

"And what if she finds out some other way? How much more would that hurt?"

Being "honest" was one thing. Telling the brutal truth was another. Was Julie a delicate girl who could be destroyed by the thought of her life beginning under the cloak of a rapist's attack? Could I risk destroying any feelings of self-worth and purpose in her life? No! I wouldn't take that risk.

Fortunately, Julie had asked no further questions about her natural father. Maybe she didn't want to embarrass me or strain our developing relationship. Still, Hal felt strongly that my reputation and integrity could be harmed with Julie if she didn't know the truth. Reluctantly I agreed to let him talk to Julie's husband. One evening we were both talking on the phone with Julie when Hal asked to speak privately with her husband, Bob.

When Bob came on, Hal asked, "Is Julie on the phone with you?"

"No," he said.

"Good, because there's something I need to tell you.

It's about Julie's conception. The circumstances surrounding it were not pretty. Lee was attacked. Can you understand what I mean?"

After a long pause, he replied, "I think I get the picture . . . or at least part of it."

"Well, we don't know if we should tell Julie this. Actually, we don't know *how* to tell her. So could we leave that up to you as her husband? You can tell her whatever and whenever you think would be best for Julie."

The silence on the other end of the phone was not golden. Finally I couldn't stand it any more. "Bob, are you there? What's your reaction?"

With deep emotion he replied, "Just think . . . that happened more than 20 years ago . . . just to give me my Julie. . . ."

As his voice trailed off, I choked up with the realization of what he had said. We were dealing with a mature, insightful Christian man who would be able to sensitively translate the circumstances of her conception to his wife.

In one of my letters to Julie I enclosed the following poem. She appreciated it and made copies for her own family:

LEGACY OF AN ADOPTED CHILD

Once there were two women
   Who never knew each other;
One you do not remember,
   The other you call mother.

One gave you a nationality,
   The other gave you a name;
One gave you the seed of talent,
   The other gave you an aim.

Two different lives shaped
   To make yours one;

116

One became your guiding star,
   The other became your sun.

One gave you emotions,
   The other calmed your fears;
One saw your first sweet smile,
   The other dried your tears.

The first gave you life and
   The second taught you to live it;
The first gave you a need for love,
   And the second was there to give it.

One gave you up,
   It was all that she could do;
The other prayed for a child,
   And God led her straight to you.

And now you ask me through your
   tears
The age-old question through the
   years:
Heredity or environment: Which
   are you the product of?
Neither, my darling, neither—
   Just two different kinds of love.

     —Anonymous

    Increasingly I wondered when Julie and I should try meeting face to face. As Hal and I discussed it, I noted that we would be in Washington D.C. for a convention the second week in February. "It will be Julie's twenty-first birthday," I told Hal. "Why don't we have her and Bob join us for a few days?"

    Hal agreed, and we proposed it to Bob and Julie, who accepted the invitation. Now that our first meeting was approaching, I had increasing apprehensions. After all, Julie had had 3½ years to adjust to the idea of finding me. But my girls had just a few weeks, and they still didn't seem overjoyed at the idea. And for me, even 20 years was not enough time to adjust to the fact that my baby was a full-grown woman about to celebrate her twenty-first birthday.

I was concerned about whether I should let her call me "Mom." Because of Pam and Sandi's initial reaction, I wanted to be cautious, though everything inside me screamed, "Yes, call me 'Mom.' I am!" But then, what if she didn't want to do that? And what if Julie didn't like me? Or what if I didn't like her? What would I do if she didn't look like me but looked more like her natural father? And how would her parents feel about this meeting? Would this interfere in the life they had nurtured so well?

Before we left for Washington, I went shopping for Julie's birthday card. I quickly noticed that none of the cards seemed to fit the occasion:

"To OUR daughter . . ."
"What a joy you've always been . . ."
"Mom and Dad are proud of you!"

There were cards that rhymed, like this:

"We gave you toys and games and
    books, we gave you a home, and
    our good looks;
We gave you advice and showed
    concern, and dear daughter, what
    did you give in return?
More love and pride than we can
    measure, and a lifetime of memories
    to treasure."

Flustered by the cards, I gave up and walked over to the infant department to buy a gift for Julie's daughter.

As I took a cute little dress to the counter, a lady next to me asked in her best social voice, "Is that for your little one?"

I felt my face flush as I stuttered, for the first time, "No, it's for my gr-gr-granddaughter!"

13

Face to Face

Despite all the excitement that surrounds the National Religious Broadcasters convention, I had a hard time concentrating. It was a constant struggle to respond intelligently as people inquired about my radio program "Reflections." Every evening as I returned to my hotel, my thoughts would drift to Julie and Bob, and I would wonder how our meeting would turn out. I was particularly curious about whether I would recognize my daughter. Could I have picked her out if she had passed me on the street? Would she look like me, or more like her natural father? My curiosity was insatiable

With our meeting less than 24 hours away, I relaxed in my hotel room and thought of how Bob and Julie were now probably preparing to leave Michigan early in the morning for the long drive to Washington. "Lord, protect them," I prayed, thinking of the harsh winter they were having further north.

The phone rang and I answered. It was Sandi and Pam. After some small talk, Pam said, "We know you're going to meet Julie tomorrow. You know that we've struggled with this, but we're feeling better about it now. We just didn't want it to disrupt our family."

Sandi continued. "But we have enough spiritual

understanding to know that this is something God has done. We don't want to interfere with His plans. It is between Him and you, really. So we have agreed that you should let her call you 'Mom' if she wants to, or do anything you feel comfortable with. We will make our adjustments. We know you love us, and we love you too."

What a relief! I told Hal the news, commenting, "God blows my mind! He comes through again just 24 hours away from D-Day. I've been humming a chorus today, and how true it is: 'He makes all things beautiful in His time.'"

"It's just that sometimes His time gets pretty close to the wire," said Hal with a grin.

I had been worried about meeting Julie while still wrestling with whether to let her call me "Mom." If I didn't, wouldn't that be the ultimate rejection she had feared all her life? It was one thing to be rejected as an infant by an unknown mother, but to be rejected as an adult by your birthmother would be worse. So I was grateful for my daughters' timely call and the relief it brought me.

The next night I returned to my room from the closing banquet of the NRB convention, decked out in my friend Alyson's sequined top. Hal was waiting for me, and as he opened the door he said, "They're here."

"Here? In our room?" I panicked.

"Next door," Hal said, pointing to the door connecting us to the adjoining room. I stared at that door for a moment, knowing that the person who was my flesh and blood was waiting behind it. "Julie called and wants to come to our room just as soon as you are ready."

"I can't meet her looking like this," I said, afraid that my flashy outfit would give her some unreal Hollywood image of me. That was not what I wanted to convey. I quickly slipped out of my fancy clothes and into a comfortable blouse and slacks. Usually these old, casual clothes eased me into a state of relaxation, but not tonight. They did nothing to ease my tensions, nor did all the mental rehearsals I had walked through in my mind as I tried to prepare for this moment.

With sweaty palms and shaking inside, I stepped over to the door and knocked. "Julie, are you in there?"

A shy voice replied, "Yes. Can we come in?"

As the door swung open, a groundswell of feelings rippled from my toes to my head. Through the door walked a woman who looked strikingly like I had at her age. Now I was embarrassed with my casual attire. How could I have known that on the other side of that connecting door Julie was dressing up for the occasion with a new black crepe dress she had bought just for this moment? She had fixed up her hair, put on a string of pearls, and dressed up the baby for her first glimpse of Grandma.

We embraced and giggled and cried all at the same time. Bob was right behind her, and Hal and I warmly greeted him and the baby he was holding in his arms. After the initial hellos, we sat down and gazed at each other through tears of joy. For a few moments we were speechless at the realization that God had coordinated our meeting. No one wanted to break the silence. I searched Julie's face for clues that might tell me what she was like. Finally I had to pinch her arm as I said, "Is this really happening?"

"Yes," she laughed, "this is really happening!" Bob kept whispering, "This is great. This is terrific! Man, this is wonderful. Praise the Lord!" Only the baby's cries for attention brought us back to reality.

After the baby's needs were met, we settled again on the sofas and I began to drink in the similarities of Julie's appearance to mine. Other than a bump on my nose caused by my father dropping me as a baby (and my wrinkles), our facial features were similar. Her dark hair and eyes and big smile made me think I was looking into a reflecting pool. Her mellow voice and giggle had a familiar ring.

We made some small talk for a while, then Julie brought out some photo albums that contained childhood memories. There were pictures of Christmases with Julie dressed in little red crinkly dresses, and Easter with a cute new spring dress to wear to church. There were pictures of her with baby toys, then tricycles and bicycles. And of course there were family pictures as I had my first glimpse of the Andersons, the special couple who had become the parents to my baby.

With every picture, Julie unraveled more of the story of the past 21 years. I learned about her two older brothers Jim and then Rick, who was now a pastor in Bakersfield, California. I discovered that her father was a construction worker who helped put together the steel framing for many Los Angeles skyscrapers. Her mother made many of Julie's clothes, something that warmed my heart, for I didn't sew. In all the photos, Julie appeared content. It was obvious that she was very secure and loved as a child.

As I saw the first pictures of Julie and Bob, I asked about their romance. "We met in a Christian coffee shop in Cheboygan," said Julie. "I was 16 years old and I went there one evening with a friend to listen to some Christian music. Bob was the emcee. He organized the music groups and introduced them. He came over to my table and started talking. Bob is eight years older than I, but we just hit it off. We started dating and then decided to get married."

"What convinced you to get married?"

"Bob and I just knew it was God's will, and we convinced my parents and they said okay."

I was impressed that for Julie it seemed so normal to let God control her life. At her age I was just trying to survive. "Bob, are you still working at the coffee shop?" I asked.

"No, I drive a truck for a nearby soft-drink bottling company. Julie, did you tell Lee about the home we're going to build?"

"We live in a mobile home on two acres about ten miles from town. We're in the woods and we're in the process of cutting the trees. We have our own little sawmill, and we plan to build a log house."

As the baby slept, the four of us lost track of time. Shortly after midnight we realized we needed to stop and get some rest. But first Bob stood and said, "I would like to say something. Lee, I would like to thank you for not aborting Julie. That might have been the most convenient thing to do. I just can't imagine living my life without her . . . and my baby." What a tender moment that was as we all embraced in a communal hug! I was so grateful no "free clinic" had been accessible to tempt me those many years ago.

The next day was Julie's twenty-first birthday, and we celebrated with one candle in a cupcake, for this was her first birthday in my life. Then we went out for dinner, and during the evening I shared my "before meeting Julie" apprehensions. "I wondered if Julie would dance into my life like some little musical comedy star. Or would she be a poor soul, depressed by her circumstances and wanting to run away? But neither one is true! You are so beautiful. You're a delight to be with!"

Julie shared that she had her own misgivings about our first meeting. "Bob and I had 3½ years to consider what we might have to deal with when we found you, and . . ." It was obvious she was a little embarrassed now to admit, "we wondered if we might find some down-and-outer and wind up having to take her into our home forever!" With that we both started giggling as we realized we had been harboring similar thoughts.

For the next few days we toured the sights of Washington. Hal had business to conduct during the day, so

Bob, Julie, the baby, and I bundled up and braved the cold to see the Capitol, the White House, the memorials around Capitol Mall, the Smithsonian Institute, and other tourist sites. "Believe it or not, this seems warm to us," Bob said one day. "Back home they're battling a couple of feet of snow."

Then Julie added, "But the real reason he's glad to be here is that this is Bob's first trip outside of Michigan!"

Most of the time we were so overwhelmed by the emotion of the experience that we couldn't do much more than giggle and pinch each other. This didn't seem real. We were overwhelmed to realize how God was faithful and powerful enough to have coordinated every detail of our lives. Many times we would wind up simply saying, "Wow! Isn't God good!" as another piece of information was placed into the puzzle.

One day during lunch I inquired about the church that Julie had attended in the San Fernando Valley before her family moved back to Michigan. It turned out to be a little church that my sister Zoe had attended on occasion. "My nieces and nephews might have attended the same Sunday school class!" I remarked.

I asked about how Julie came to Christ, and she replied, "I've always felt close to God. I received Christ in that little church when I was a small girl, and then I made a deeper commitment to Him after Bob and I were married."

Julie's family moved to Michigan when she was in junior high school. That was when her activity in music had increased. "I'll bet you sing alto," I said.

"Yes!" she smiled. "I suppose that's what you sing too. What kind of singing have you done?" Julie inquired.

"Well, I've sung in choirs. After my conversion I sang some solos in churches. I've always enjoyed doing musical comedies in school and community theater productions. The highlight of my career was when I played Golde, the Mama, in a stage production of

'Fiddler on the Roof.' I got to sing some good songs in that."

"Sunrise, Sunset!"

"And 'Do You Love Me?' " I sang, imitating a Jewish accent in the scene where Reb Tevya and Golde discover that they really do love each other—after 25 years. And after 20 years Julie and I were discovering the same thing!

Julie laughed at my imitation of a Jewish Mama, then told me about her involvement in church music. "I sing in our church choir, and a trio, plus a special ensemble. I haven't had your stage experience, except for some seasonal productions in our church. I think I got my greatest joy when we would visit old people's homes and I see them cheer up as we would sing."

One day as we were walking on the Washington Mall, I mustered up the courage to ask Julie how she felt about her natural father.

"Bob told me what you said about my conception," she said.

"And, uh, how did you feel about that?" I asked.

She hesitated before saying, "For three days it was very difficult for me. I felt deeply hurt."

I paused, then ventured, "What happened after three days?"

"I finally decided that God was the One who wanted me to be born."

We walked tearfully in silence for a few moments as I contemplated what she had said. Finally I remarked, "It sounds like you understand the message of Psalm 139, that God formed us in the womb and knew us before we were born. I think we've been reading the same Book!"

"Yes, that's it! The Bible has convinced me that I wasn't an accident, that God intended for me to live for a purpose."

I responded, "And one of those purposes was that I would come to know Him." It was a thrill to further explain to her the joy I experienced as she was growing in my body, for at the same time the life of Christ was growing in me by leaps and bounds.

It seemed natural for Julie to start calling me "Mom" and even "Grandma" when talking to her baby girl. I was holding Casey in my arms as we stood in line at the White House when a friendly woman behind me asked, "Who is this?" Awkwardly I responded, "This is my . . . granddaughter." As the words of my mouth hit my ears, the reality of it jarred me. It really was true!

On the last night of our visit, as we were eating dinner, Bob asked, "What is the meaning of all this, Lee? Why would God decide to do this?"

I sensed that Bob had something specific in mind, so I didn't try to answer. "Do you have any ideas?" I prompted.

"I don't think God arranged and coordinated all of this just to satisfy our curiosity. There must be more to it. You're a Christian speaker and author. I'm wondering if God has allowed this because He wanted you to write about it. Maybe this story could give people hope as they see the faithfulness of God."

"It definitely is a demonstration of God's faithfulness," I remarked. "Maybe He does want me to write a book. We'll have to wait and see. Right now I just want to enjoy it all." There was another concern to consider. "Julie, how do your parents feel about this now that we've actually met?"

"I think they feel good about it," Julie said. "They realize that you don't intend to make a big interruption in their lives. I think they're relieved and feel we can have a good, meaningful relationship."

It had been a wonderful time together, and our parting was tearful. As we packed Bob and Julie and the baby into the car for their trip home, I asked Julie, "Where do we go from here?"

"Let's keep in touch and see what happens," said Julie. "Maybe sometime you can meet my family."

"That would mean a lot, if they're comfortable with it."

Then we hugged and watched them pull out of the driveway. As I caught one last wave from Julie, I whispered, "Thank You, Lord, for letting me catch a glimpse of *Your* side of the tapestry."

14

Fitting the Pieces Together

We were nearly two hours out of Washington D.C. The flight attendants were collecting dinner trays and preparing for the in-flight movie. Hal was busy next to me catching up on his paperwork and dictation. As I looked out the window, my mind was a blur. For the last few days I had seen an "impossible dream" come true. A part of my past that I had considered closed had come back, not to haunt me but to bless me. God had turned the weaving over and allowed me a glimpse at the finished side.

As I thought of my experience, a song kept going through my mind. It was from John Fischer's musical "The New Covenant," and I had memorized the lyrics because they meant so much to me.

We all get hurt.
We always seem to end up
face down in the dirt.
And hounded by the pain,
We just remain
Satisfied to be hurt again.

We close our minds to the meaning
in the madness that we find.

We prefer to hide out,
Rarely try to find out
Just what pain is all about.

But if there's one thing you need to know,
It's that hurtin' only makes you grow,
and the pain you feel
is the first step to being healed.

But there's one thing you need to do,
It's to get your eyes off you,
Place them on the Lord,
And He'll make pain an *open door*.*

What was the message in my meeting Julie? This song expressed it. We all get hurt at some time in our lives, and we must choose whether or not to see God's meaning in the madness. As I reflected on my spiritual walk, I truly had dropped my self-pity look and placed my eyes on God. He had indeed caused my pain to become an open door to a vital relationship with Him, and now He was opening doors of useful service for Him.

I thought of the speaking engagements that were already scheduled for me over the next few months. I would conduct retreats and speak to women's groups, plus record a daily radio program. Everyone in my audiences suffered her own hurts. Maybe they hadn't endurd a rape and had to give a child up for adoption, but many could express much deeper hurts and disappointments than mine. They were suffering the pain of divorce, or a chronic health problem, or a retarded child, or financial setback, or rejection by a loved one or friend . . . the list was endless. Some were victims, others had caused their own pain. What had I learned that might encourage all these people?

I grabbed my satchel, pulled out a notebook and Bible, and began to write down my thoughts. On the top of a blank page I wrote "Missing Pieces." I had thought back to the awful day when my life looked like a complex puzzle, with several important pieces missing. I had wondered then if God could show me how to get it together again.

The wonder of my meeting with Julie was that an original missing piece had been put back in place. Yet not everyone is so fortunate. Not everyone can say that his gaping hole has been filled. What could I say to those people?

I could say that my life was complete *before* I saw Julie. Sure, she had been a missing piece in my life, but that hole had been plugged up even before I met her. What material had I used to fill this hole? I jotted down some of the key ingredients.

Piece number one: SURRENDER. It had all begun at the Billy Graham Crusade when I received Christ as my Savior. In a way I hadn't really understood at the time, I had surrendered my life to God's control. I pictured it now as something like the war movies I'd seen where the soldiers wave a white flag, throw down their weapons, and surrender to the winning side. That's what I had needed to do—to lay down my life and give up to God's purposes so He could put the pieces of my puzzle together.

Throughout life we all experience difficulties and must learn to surrender our "unfair" protests, our "I don't deserve this" feelings. We must also relinquish our anger, our "get even" feelings, and our self-pity. Spiritual and emotional growth is the result of this yielding.

Piece number two: COMMITMENT. In committing my rape experience to the Lord I couldn't imagine at the time that I was also committing a little life forming inside me. Soon I discovered that committing our experiences doesn't cancel their effects, but it does input the consequences to the divine computer for coordination of their outcome. I read in Paul's second letter to Timothy: "For which cause I also suffer these things; nevertheless I am not ashamed, for I know whom I have believed and am persuaded that *he is able* to keep that which I have *committed* unto him."[1]

I thought again of my battle with the social worker. I was committed to doing all I could to place my child in a Christian home. And God had honored that commitment, working where I couldn't work in order to answer my prayer. So I would encourage people to commit not just "a hardship piece" of their lives to God, but their whole puzzling life—their finances, career, marriage, future.

Piece number three: FORGIVENESS. The memory of that dingy motel room remained vivid. There I had realized that I could hold grudges justifiably against all who had hurt me, but be destroyed in the process. Or I could obey God and forgive those who had caused me pain, and God would forgive me of my sins. What peace had flooded me that morning as I released all the pent-up bitterness! For the first time I had truly experienced the freedom of an unhindered relationship with God. It is this forgiving spirit which enables the Lord to "work all things together for good."[2]

Piece number four: Assume YOU'RE A TRUSTEE. Now it was no longer "Why me, God?" but "God, are You trusting me with this?" He was not giving me more than I could handle, but was providing me with all I needed to endure the situation. *What can't be cured can be endured*. As God did with Moses' mother, He was using the situation for my good and for the good of other people. When I discovered I was pregnant, I realized that God had entrusted me with that situation, and I didn't want to let Him down. God wants to deliver us *in* and *through* our troubles, not *out of* them.

Piece number five: THANKSGIVING. My circumstances didn't become rosy after I accepted the fact that I was a trustee over them. I was still pregnant. I had gone to live with Uncle Howard in less-than-ideal conditions. But in that situation I had learned that there was plenty that I could be thankful for. With that grateful spirit I found I was better able to cope in the difficult circumstances. Now I could count my blessings instead of sheep.

Piece number six: Realizing that there is PURPOSE IN PAIN. There is a method to all this madness. The birth of my baby was my first glimpse into the purpose of God through my pain. The Old Testament Joseph interpreted God through all his injustices and saw method in the madness. Like Joseph, my circumstances had turned out to be a blessing in disguise. I turned to Luke 11 and read these words: "Suppose one of you fathers is asked by his son for a fish; he will not give him a snake instead of a fish, will he? Or if he is asked for an egg, he will not give him a scorpion, will he?"[3]

At one time I, like many Christians, felt victimized, thinking instead of receiving fish and eggs, I had been given snakes and scorpions. I had reacted with a normal question: "Why, God?" But over time I had learned a better question: "Lord, I know You have some hidden purpose in allowing me to have this problem. Will You go through it with me?"

That's what Paul did when he had his "thorn in the flesh" problem. Three times he asked God to remove it, but then he learned that God had a reason for it: first, to keep him from exalting himself, and second, to demonstrate God's power in Paul's weakness. Through that experience Paul learned an important lesson that helped him in many situations: "Therefore I am well content with weaknesses, with insults, with distresses, with persecutions, with difficulties, for Christ's sake; for when I am weak, then I am strong."[4]

Life is not simple; it is extremely complex nowadays, and I wouldn't want to minimize the pain and the injustice that people suffer. I realized, too, there were no instant answers; mine took over 20 years. Yet before we know all the reasons why, we can know the *peace* of God for our missing *pieces*.

As I looked over my paper, I realized that some people would object, saying that they were not victims. I thought of a counseling session I had recently where the woman had protested, "I'm suffering because of my own stupid choices. I'm not a victim. My problems are my own fault."

I had responded, "But it's the outcome that counts. If you surrender and commit yourself to God, He'll work with you in spite of your mistakes. You cannot make any blunder big enough for God to get frustrated and cry, 'Oh, no! I can't work around that.' There is nothing in your past which can put you out of commission. God will weave even that ugly experience into the tapestry to accomplish His plan for your life. When we submit ourselves to God, we no longer need to labor under the guilt and shame of our poor choices. I have Christian friends who have repented of an extramarital affair, a willful disobedience, an abortion . . . all kinds of errors. They are now living victorious lives."

As the captain began his approach into the Los Angeles International Airport, I shared my new message with Hal. He responded, "You know, it's crystal clear who the hero of this story is. It's not you or Julie. There was only one main character who could possibly have pulled this whole story together. It was God."

"You know, Bob was right," I said. "This reunion was not just for our sakes. It must be that we're to tell the story of the faithfulness and power of God in order to encourage others. Writing this message has shown me that I will have to write the story of this missing piece in my life. Maybe I can exhort others to not *waste* their sorrows but to turn their stumbling-block experiences into stepping-stones."

In one sense I was tempted to think that everything was now set into place in my life. But that really wasn't true. There were still many unresolved questions . . . missing pieces. I had not yet met Julie's parents. How were they really feeling? My daughters had come a long way in accepting Julie, but they had not yet encountered her. They still needed time to adjust to this idea. Everything was not all neatly wrapped up Cinderella-style. In a sense I was glad I didn't know the future, for I would either desire it or dread it.

I thought of the verse from the book of Deuteronomy that says, "The secret things belong to the Lord our God, but the things revealed belong to us . . ."[5] Some aspects of my experiences were still a secret, but God had revealed a few things to me through my pain. They didn't come overnight. It wasn't like instant pudding, or instant coffee, or instant banking. We are so used to snapping our fingers and finding the right combination, and poof!—instant change. But our "formulas" don't always work with God. That's why He supplies *internal* answers even when our *external* questions remain. God wants victorious victims and He can use scarred counselors.

More than my meager schooling, my years in the school of hard knocks and the lessons I had learned there now qualified me to help other people as a wounded healer. My injuries were now scars, for the wounds of my past were healed. But the comfort the Lord gave me was what He wanted me to share with other people also.

As the plane touched down, I thought again of the chorus "He makes all things beautiful in His time." It had been the right time for God to masterfully restore my missing piece. And now I knew more deeply than ever before that God can make all things beautiful in *every* hurting life. He will supply His peace for our missing pieces.

Scripture References

CHAPTER 3

1. Psalm 37:4,5 KJV.
2. 2 Corinthians 11:24,25 NASB.
3. 2 Corinthians 4:8,9 NASB.
4. Proverbs 3:5,6 NIV.

CHAPTER 4

1. Matthew 6:9–12 KJV.
2. Matthew 6:14,15 KJV.
3. Matthew 26:39 KJV.
4. Matthew 27:46 KJV.

CHAPTER 5

1. Philippians 4:8 KJV.
2. 1 Thessalonians 5:18 NASB.
3. Colossians 3:17 NASB.
4. Philippians 4:6 NASB.
5. Romans 8:31,35,37–39 NASB.

CHAPTER 6

1. Psalm 139:13–16 TLB.
2. Genesis 45:5 NASB.
3. Genesis 45:7 NASB.

4. Genesis 50:20 NIV.
5. Jeremiah 29:11 NIV.

CHAPTER 7

1. John 19:11 NASB.

CHAPTER 9

1. Psalm 118:24 NIV.

CHAPTER 14

1. 2 Timothy 1:12 KJV.
2. Romans 8:28 KJV.
3. Luke 11:11,12 NASB.
4. 2 Corinthians 12:10 NASB.
5. Deuteronomy 29:29 NASB.

ABOUT THE AUTHOR

LEE EZELL has appeared on numerous television and radio programs, including Robert Schuller's "Hour of Power," CBS and ABC Network News, Sally Jesse Raphael, and James Dobson's "Focus on the Family." She is also host of her own nationally syndicated radio show, "Reflections."

She has been the subject of articles carried by Associated Press and United Press International, and is a member of the National Speakers Association. She regularly addresses women's organizations and churches across the country, as well as government agencies.

Ezell is the author of two award-winning books, *The Cinderella Syndrome* and *The Missing Piece*.

She resides in southern California with her husband, Hal, the U.S. Western Regional Commissioner of Immigration, and her two daughters.